20 SITUATIONAL CONVERSATIONS
IN UP-TO-DATE INTERNATIONAL
CONSTRUCTION CONTRACTING BUSINESS

# 最新国际工程承包情景会话 20 讲

吴之昕　刘鸣笛　著

中国建筑工业出版社

图书在版编目（CIP）数据

最新国际工程承包情景会话 20 讲 = 20 SITUATIONAL CONVERSATIONS IN UP-TO-DATE INTERNATIONAL CONSTRUCTION CONTRACTING BUSINESS / 吴之昕，刘鸣笛著 . —北京：中国建筑工业出版社，2020.12
ISBN 978-7-112-25798-0

Ⅰ.①最… Ⅱ.①吴… ②刘… Ⅲ.①国际承包工程—基本知识 Ⅳ.① F746.18

中国版本图书馆 CIP 数据核字（2020）第 267585 号

责任编辑：张鹏伟　程素荣
责任校对：芦欣甜

## 最新国际工程承包情景会话 20 讲
20 SITUATIONAL CONVERSATIONS IN UP-TO-DATE
INTERNATIONAL CONSTRUCTION CONTRACTING BUSINESS
吴之昕　刘鸣笛　著
\*
中国建筑工业出版社出版、发行（北京海淀三里河路 9 号）
各地新华书店、建筑书店经销
北京雅盈中佳图文设计公司制版
北京京华铭诚工贸有限公司印刷
\*
开本：850 毫米 ×1168 毫米　1/32　印张：$7\frac{1}{2}$　字数：187 千字
2021 年 3 月第一版　2021 年 3 月第一次印刷
定价：**55.00** 元
ISBN 978-7-112-25798-0
（36584）

**版权所有　翻印必究**
如有印装质量问题，可寄本社图书出版中心退换
（邮政编码 100037）

# 序

2003年，我为《工程承包实用英语会话》一书作了序。弹指一挥17年已过，在这不算长的时间里中国已快速发展成为世界第二大经济体。中国的国际工程承包行业也蓬勃发展，业务遍及世界各大洲，项目规模越做越大，实施模式正在快速地向诸如BOT、PPP等层出不穷的高端模式发展，中国的国际工程承包迈入了一个新的阶段。在此期间，我国的国际工程承包企业积极实施国家"走出去战略"，并响应"一带一路"倡议，大力推动国际贸易的发展，也为我国出口创汇、增强国际影响力做出了不可磨灭的贡献。

然而在此过程中，由于国际工程承包事业的突飞猛进的发展，也突显了懂英语、精业务的国际化人才的短缺；同时也缺乏适合业务一线人员所需的培训教材问题。为适应我国国际承包业务的发展，本书作者急广大从事国际工程承包工作的人员之所急，根据其在此17年间从事海外国际工程及市场开拓积累的丰富经验和亲身体会，撰写了《工程承包实用英语会话》一书的姊妹篇——《最新国际工程承包情景会话20讲》一书，可谓"雪中送炭"弥补了这个空缺。

本书虽然仍是以特定场景下的会话形式为载体，但绝不是在《工程承包实用英语会话》基础上的简单修改，而是根据我国国际工程承包企业当前在海外开拓及执行项目所面临的实际问题而重构的一个体系，它具有非常鲜明的特色：

第一是覆盖项目的全生命周期——本书模拟了一个在 A 国的 BOT 公路项目，涵盖了其从项目前期开发、合同谈判，到项目的施工、运维及移交整个二十多年的生命周期的各个阶段，使读者整体了解一个实际项目的运作过程；

第二则是实用性强——本书没有采用教科书式的教学，而是模拟业务中通常发生的场景，设计了鲜活的人物及极具有现实指导意义的对话；

第三是用语规范准确——本书英语会话符合英语国家的使用习惯，专业术语符合国际通用标准，显示了作者深厚的中英文语言功底，给予读者良好的示范效应。

归纳起来，我觉得本书有几个印象深刻和难能可贵之处：

本书两位作者都亲身在海外工程承包一线积累了十余年实战经验，难能可贵；

本书的主题紧扣工程承包模式升级、适应我国对外工程承包业已由大转强的需要，难能可贵；

本书不但以对话的形式呈现规范的国际工程商务英语，更难能可贵的是给出了应对海外 BOT 项目运作中各种难题值得称道的真经实招；

更为难能可贵的特点是本书两位作者，一位年逾古稀、一位方值而立之年，老少合璧、薪火传承，让我们看到我国对外工程承包事业兴旺发达、后继有人也。

本书既可以作为我国从事国际工程承包业务人员的一本入门教材，也可以作为业务实操的参考书。在我国国际工程承包行业发展，方兴未艾的当下，此书的出版发行，实具十分重要而积极的意义。故此推荐，并为之序。

建设部科学技术委员会顾问
瑞典皇家工程科学院外籍院士

*许溶烈*

2020年5月10日于北京

# PREFACE

In 2003, I wrote a preface for the book *Practical Oral English for Construction & Contracting Business*. From that time, 17 years have passed with a flick of the finger, while China has rapidly developed into the second largest economy in the world, and China's international construction & contracting industry has also been growing boomingly and entered a new stage. China's international construction & contracting business has spread to all continents of the world, the scale of projects is getting larger as well, and the projects implementation is rapidly upgrading to the high-end model, such as BOT and PPP. During this period, China's international construction & contracting enterprises actively implemented the national "Going Global" strategy and followed the "Belt and Road" initiative, vigorously promoted international economic and trade cooperation, and made an indelible contribution to China's foreign exchange earnings and enhancement of China's international influence.

In this process however, due to the rapid development of the international construction & contracting business, it also exposed the shortage of internationalized talents who are proficient in both foreign language and business, as well as the lack of training materials required by front-line employees under the new situation. In order to adapt to the development of China's international construction & contracting business, the authors of this book are eager to meet the urgent needs of the vast number of personnel engaged in international construction & contracting industry. Based on their rich experience in international projects and overseas market development during the last 17 years, they wrote the companion volume of *Practical Oral English for Construction & Contracting Business—20 Situational Conversations in Up-to-date International Construction Contracting Business* to make up for this vacancy, which provides timely help just like the Chinese idiom "sending charcoal in snowy weather".

Although the book is still based on the conversational form under specific scenarios, it is not just a simple modification based on the previous book, but a system reconstructed according to the practical problems faced by China's international construction & contracting enterprises during their current overseas development and implementation of projects. It has very distinctive features:

Firstly, it covers the whole life cycle of the project–this book simulates a BOT highway project in Country A, covering all stages of its life cycle of more than 20 years: from market development, contract negotiation, to project construction, operation & maintenance and handover, so that readers can understand the process of an actual project as a whole.

The second is strong practicality–this book does not adopt the form of a textbook, but simulates the typical scenes that usually happen in actual business, and designs vivid characters and very instructive dialogues.

The third is the accurate and standardized terminology-the English conversations in this book conform to the usage habits of English-speaking countries, and the professional terms conform to the international standards, which show the author's profound Chinese and English language skills, and offer a good demonstration to the readers.

In summary, I think this book has several impressive and commendable points to mention:

The two authors of this book have personally accumulated more than ten years of forefront experience in international construction & contracting business, which is commendable.

The theme of this book is closely related to the upgrading of contracting model and adapted to the need for a large and strong, industry of China's international construction & contracting.

This book not only presents the standard business English in international construction & contracting business in the form of dialogue, but also presents the commendable real solutions to various problems during the operation of overseas BOT projects.

One more commendable feature is that the two authors of this book, one is over seventy years of age and the other is just over his thirties. The combination of the two shows the inheritance of the industry. It is foreseeable that China's international construction &

contracting business will be prosperous with successors.

This book can be used not only as an entry-level textbook for personnel engaged in international construction & contracting business, but also as a reference book for actual business practice. In the current development of China's international construction & contracting industry, the publication of this book is of great and positive significance. Thus I hereby recommend the book and write this preface.

Advisor, Committee for Science & Technology,
Ministry of Construction, PRC
Foreign Academician, Royal Swedish
Academy of Engineering Sciences

**Xu Ronglie**

May 10, 2020 in Beijing

# 前　言

《最新国际工程承包情景会话20讲》原打算是在2019年春天就付印出版的，但当时为了赶在我国对外工程承包40年之际交付《国际工程商务能力培训系列教材》的全套书稿，就把本书的编写工作放下了。一晃就到了2020年春天，我的《最新国际工程承包情景会话20讲》书稿是完成了，但恰如17年之前我完成本书姐妹篇《工程承包实用英语会话》时"撞上"了"非典"一样，这次则在庚子之春又"撞上"了"新冠肺炎"。

我着手编写《工程承包实用英语会话》那本口袋书的2001年，正值我们中国加入世界贸易组织WTO进入冲刺阶段。越来越多的国内承包商响应国家的"走出去"战略，积极参与对外承包工程的业务。2001年年底，中国正式加入WTO。当年中国对外承包工程完成营业额为89亿美元，占ENR全球225家最大承包商国际市场营业总额的8.36%，在各国际工程承包服务提供国里排在第8位。当时中国对外承包工程的主要模式从劳务分包向施工承包转型，以成套设备出口带动的EPC工程承包模式刚刚起步。时光荏苒，到我着手编写《最新国际工程承包情景会话20讲》的2018年，我们中国对外承包工程完成营业额达到1189.7亿美元，占ENR全球250家最大承包商国际市场营业总额的24.4%，中国已经发展成为全球国际工程承包服务的第一大提供国。17年中，中国对外承包工程的模式从施工承包、EPC设计施工总承包、F+EPC融资加设计施工总承包发展到BOT建造—运营—转让、DBFOT设计—建设—融资—运营—转让、PPP政府与私营机构合作等最新工程承包模式。原来以施工承包为背景编写的《工程承包实用英语会话》已经远远满足不了形势发展的需要，广大对外承包工程工作者迫切盼望能有一本与国际工程承包新形势、新模式、新实践相对接的英语口袋书随身相伴，这便是我们编写本书的动因。

《工程承包实用英语会话》出版后的17年里，我自己也有了更加丰富的经历，从房地产公司董事长职务上跳槽到我国首个PPP模式的大型公建项目"鸟巢"，担任施工方的总工程师，获得了与来自世界各国的建筑师、工程师、咨询师直接进行业务交流的难得机会；接着远赴非洲工作八年，承建当时世界上单个合同金额最大的新城开发项目并开拓周边国家的基本建设工程市场，从事包括房屋建筑、交通道路、供水排水、污水处理、输变电等多种性质的工程，先后有幸面见、拜会了十余个国家的元首或政府首脑，有幸向近百位各国部长作商务和技术演示、汇报，有幸与数百位各国政府官员、投资商、开发商、会计师、银行家、设计师、监理工程师、律师、港口及海关工作人员共同工作或探讨，并与其中很多人结成了好朋友。这17年的经历让我进一步开阔了视野、积累了经验，给了我着手编写本书的底气。

于是我邀请了我的年轻同事、北京外国语大学国际经贸专业毕业生刘鸣笛共同编写本书。他年纪轻轻，已经有近十年的海外工程承包的工作经验，并曾担任名列ENR国际承包商第

43位的中国承包商的非洲区市场部经理。我们在整理总结自身工程经验的同时，拜访请教了多位国际工程投资建设的专家，查阅了大量国内外的专业资料，两个人反复互审初稿、数易其稿，并恭请英国仲裁师朋友作了把关审阅。

为了使《最新国际工程承包情景会话20讲》能更加贴近实际，能为我国海外建设者提供实实在在的工作借鉴和语言支持，我们设想以一个海外基础设施投资项目为背景，以对话的形式完整地反映项目从市场调研、客户接洽、可研策划、融资签约、实施运营直至转让移交全过程的关键活动。为此，在本书的策划、编写中我们遵循了以下的思路：

1. 突出背景项目的代表性。据我们了解，在我国参与的海外基础设施投资项目中，仍以BOT模式的居多。根据ENR对国际承包商250强所完成营业额业务领域分布的统计，交通运输基础设施排在各领域之首，而在各类交通运输基础设施项目中又以公路项目的数量最多。因此，我们选择了以BOT模式下的海外高速公路项目作为本书的背景。

2. 瞄准项目成败的关键环节。作为一本口袋书，本书仍参照其姐妹篇《工程承包实用英语会话》共计三章、20课的框架，每一章对应项目运作的一个阶段，每一课对应运作的一个环节。海外基础设施投资项目的全过程如果要展开分解的话，可以罗列出来上百个环节，需要从中筛选出最关键的20个不可或缺的环节。诚然，在《工程承包实用英语会话》里已经涉及施工承包模式下投标、报价、质量、安全、计量、索赔等关键环节，仍然是BOT项目运作中不可或缺的，但本书必须把关注点聚焦到很多海外建设者尚不熟悉的 BOT 项目特有的、至关重要的运作环节上来。有些看似并非工程建设核心业务但事关项目成败的活动，比如"征地"、"安防部署"、"履行社会责任"等环节，恰恰是中国承包商实施海外投资项目容易疏忽的关键点，本书特别将他们列进来。

3. 抓住项目运作的纠结点、冲突点、风险点。本书每一课针对项目运作的某一环节安排一到两个对话来展现这一环节涉及的主要活动，但绝不是平铺直叙地罗列一个工作清单。我们特别注意回忆和搜集在项目运作中自身或者同行曾经遇到过的"坑"和"雷"，曾经碰过的"钉"和绊过我们的"石"，与利益相关方曾经发生过的纠葛或冲突，通过适当的方式隐含在对话里，给读者以警示，同时又把解决这些问题的应对措施包含在对话里，给读者以借鉴。

4. 展示中国承包商的成功实践及其获得的积极反响。在国家"走出去"战略和"一带一路"倡议的指引下，我国的对外工程承包企业在五大洲都有相当成功的实践。习近平总书记在非洲视察本书作者投身建设的新城项目时告诫在非洲工作的中国承包商"先予后取，多予少取"。笔者亲身践行了习主席的上述指示，并感受到非洲人民对我们工作的肯定和赞赏。我们真心希望拿这些积极的作为和反响与广大读者分享。

5. 设定恰当的情节和角色。为了通过对话清晰、简明地阐述项目运行某一环节的工作要点，我们曾对不少情节和人物角色作了反复推敲和调整，以保证需要阐明的要点能够在适当的语境下、通过适当的角色表达出来。

6. 把握好专业语汇严谨性和口语表达流畅性之间的平衡。本书大部分章节都会涉及不少工程技术、运营管理、商务税务以及政府法规方面的专业语汇。在编写过程中，我们一方面始终坚持专业陈述的严谨、准确，另一方面力求对话语句的自然顺畅。

本书由吴之昕策划，由吴之昕、刘鸣笛合作编写，由英国特许仲裁师、工程师 Niall Lawless 先生审定，由 Clayton Rabenda 先生、Marco Denti 先生、Kaddour Chelabi 先生，Jesse Michael Young 先生、翟田田先生、陈玉帅先生、胡根先生、杜心月女士和作者共同朗读录音。鉴于我们自身的水平有限，对海外基础设施投资项目的理解尚欠专深，本书一定还存在不少错误和缺失，恳请业内专家和广大读者予以批评指正。

在本书完稿向出版社交付之际，我要衷心感谢许溶烈老总一直以来对我的教导和鼓励，并先后为《工程承包实用英语会话》及本书写序；我要感谢赵宏先生、张稚华女士、钟海祥先生在海外基础设施投资方面向我传授经验；我要感谢林峰先生、宋亮先生为本书的编写提供有益的资料。我要特别感谢我的英国朋友 Niall Lawless 先生对本书作了细致、专业、精准的审定。

吴之昕

2020 年 2 月 22 日

# FOREWORD

*20 Situational Conversations In Up-to-date International Construction Contracting Business* was originally intended to be published in Spring of 2019. To commemorate the $40^{th}$ Anniversary of China's Foreign Construction Contracting Businesses, I was asked to develop a set of reference manuscripts *Series Training Textbooks of International Contracting Commercial Competencies* and the writing of this book was rescheduled. The Spring of 2020 arrived in a flash, and the manuscript *20 Situational Conversations In Up-to-date International Construction Contracting Business* is completed. But just as I had bumped into SARS 17 years ago when I finished its companion volume *Practical Oral English for Construction Contracting Business*, this time in the Spring of the year of Gengzi, I have bumped into COVID-19.

At the end of 2001, when I started writing the pocket book *Practical Oral English for Construction Contracting Business*, China was concluding its accession to the World Trade Organization. More and more Chinese qualified contractors were encouraged by the country's "Going Global" strategy to explore opportunities for overseas construction and contracting business. At the end of 2001, China formally joined the WTO. In that year, the total overseas turnover of

Chinese contractors was $8.9 billion, which accounting for 8.36% of the total revenue of ENR's 225 top international contractors in the global market, and China was ranked eighth among the countries providing international contracting services. At that time China's main mode of overseas contracting activity was transforming from labour subcontracting to construction contracting. Meanwhile the EPC turnkey contracting model, which was driven by complete sets of equipment export, was just starting. Time flies. In 2018, when I started to write this book *20 Situational Conversations In Up-to-date International Construction Contracting Business*, the total overseas revenue of Chinese contractors reached $118.97 billion, accounting for 24.4% of the total revenue of ENR's 250 Top International Contractors in the global market, and China had become the world's number one provider of international construction contracting services. In the past 17 years, China's overseas construction contracting model has developed from construction only, to EPC, F+EPC to BOT, DBFOT, PPP and other contracting models. The booklet *Practical Oral English for Construction Contracting Business* originally conceived in the context of construction contracting, does not meet the needs of the current market. Chinese contractors are eager to have an English pocket book which is suitable for the new reality, the new models and new practices in overseas construction contracting. Their needs motivated me to write this book.

In the past 17 years since the publication of *Practical Oral

*English for Construction & Contracting Business*, my experience and involvement with overseas contracting has been rich and diverse. I have job-hopped from acting as chairman of a real estate company, to the role of chief engineer of the contractor who built the "Bird's Nest", which was China's first large-scale public building developed using the PPP model. I was privileged to work with some of the best architects, engineers and consultants from across the globe. After that I worked in Africa for eight years, undertaking the development of a new town which involved the construction of housing, roads, water supply & drainage system, sewage treatment plant, power transmission & transformation system and other types of systems. At that time this new town project was the world's largest single contract sum and it allowed me to explore the capital construction market in the neighbouring countries. I had the honor of meeting with presidents or premiers of more than 10 different countries, and the privilege of delivering business & technical presentations and reports to nearly 100 ministers of various countries. I have enjoyed being engaged in discussions or working with hundreds of government officials, investors, developers, accountants, bankers, designers, supervisors, lawyers, port and customs officials, etc., and I have made good friends with many of them. The last 17 years have enabled me to accumulate valuable experience further broadening my global outlook. This has emboldened and encouraged me to start writing this book.

So I invited my young colleague Liu Mingdi, an international trade & economics graduate from Beijing Foreign Studies University, to cooperate with me to make the book the best possible. Despite his youth, he has accumulated ten years' experience as an overseas contractor, and he has also served as the Africa Region Marketing Department manager for a Chinese contractor which is ranked 43$^{rd}$ among ENR 250 top international contractors. While documenting and summarizing our own contracting experience, we visited and consulted with many experts in the circle of international infrastructure investment and development, and reviewed a large number of professional materials from China and abroad. We reviewed each other's first drafts on an ongoing basis which resulted in improvements and modifications. We invited my UK arbitrator friend Niall Lawless to proofread the final text.

In order to connect *20 Situational Conversations In Up-to-date International Construction Contracting Business* to reality, providing practical reference and language support for the staff of overseas contractors, we envisage an overseas infrastructure investment project as the background, and organize the text in a form of dialogues which fully reflects all the project key activities from market research, customer lobbying, feasibility study, planning, financing, agreement signing, construction and operation, and concluding with transfer of the built asset. In the conception and development of this book, we embraced the following concepts:

1. To choose the most representative project. As the text background Chinese contractors have told us that the majority of overseas infrastructure investment projects are undertaken on a BOT basis. According to ENR's statistics on the distribution of the turnover in various engineering fields achieved by the 250 top international contractors, transportation infrastructure ranks first in all fields; and among transportation infrastructure projects, highway occupies the largest proportion. Therefore, we chose a highway project using the BOT model as the background project for this book.

2. To aim at the key segments that make or break a project. As a pocket book, this text uses the same framework of its companion volume *Practical Oral English for Construction & Contracting Business* with "3 chapters & 20 lessons", each chapter corresponds to one of the stages of the project and each lesson connects one of the important links in the project chain. If the whole process of an overseas infrastructure investment project is decomposed, we could list hundreds of smaller links. But we have chosen the 20 most critical and indispensable links as the background for the dialog. We submit that the key project activities referred to in the sister text *Practical Oral English for Construction & Contracting Business* such as bidding, quotation, quality control, safety, payment measurement, claim. remain indispensable in BOT projects. However, this book focuses on the crucial operational aspects of BOT projects which many overseas builders may be unfamiliar with. We have included some activities

that might seem peripheral to construction but concerning project success or failure such as "land acquisition", "security deployment" and "fulfilling social responsibility".

3. To stick to the problematic point, conflict point, risk point of the project operation. Each lesson in this book includes one or two dialogues for each link in the project operation chain to illustrate the main activities involved, but not simply in a manner similar to a task list. Special effort has been devoted to collect and retell "traps" and "mines" that we and our counterparts have encountered during overseas project development and operation. We show you "thorns" that have pricked us and "stones" which we have stumbled over, and disputes or conflicts that have occurred between the stakeholders. To forewarn our readers, such obstacles are implied into the dialogues in an appropriate manner; meanwhile for the readers benefit and learning the dialogues present countermeasures which solve the problems that arise.

4. To present the successful practices of Chinese contractors and the positive feedback received. Under the guidance of the national strategy of "Going Global" and the "the Belt and Road" Initiative, Chinese foreign contracting enterprises are performing successfully in many continents. The President Xi Jinping told Chinese contractors working in Africa to "give first and take later, give more and take less" when he was inspecting a new town project in Africa which the writers of this book devoted to. We have followed

President Xi's above instruction and have experienced firsthand the appreciation and recognition of our work by the African people. We sincerely hope to share these positive experiences and responses with our readers.

5. To create and refine the characters and the scenarios through role-play. By doing this we aim to clearly and concisely illustrate the key points of a certain link in the project operation chain through character dialogue.

6. To strike a balance between the fluency of spoken language and the rigor of professional terminology. Most chapters of this book cover a wide range of engineering technology, operational management, commerce, taxation and government regulations. In the process of writing, we always adhered to the requirements and professional rigor of real world working, and at the same time, we have strived to ensure the natural fluency of dialogues with professional language.

The book was planned by Wu Zhixin and co-written by Wu Zhixin and Liu Mingdi, and it has been reviewed by UK Chartered Arbitrator & Engineer Mr. Niall Lawless. The text recording was read aloud by Mr. Clayton Rabenda, Mr. Marco Denti, Mr. Kaddour Chelabi, Mr. Jesse Michael Young, Mr. Tiantian Zhai, Mr. Claudio Chen, Mr. William Hoo, Ms Cher Du and the authors. Where any reader feels that the book could be improved, the writers will gratefully welcome constructive criticism and suggestions for improvement.

As we deliver the book to the publisher, I would like to sincerely thank Mr. Xu Ronglie who has given me constant encouragement, guidance and support. I would like to thank Mr. Zhao Hong, Mrs. Zhang Zhihua and Mr. Zhong Haixiang for generously sharing their considerable experience of overseas infrastructure investment projects. I would like to thank Mr. Lin Feng and Mr. Song Liang for providing useful information for the preparation of this book. I particularly want to thank my UK friend Chartered Arbitrator & Engineer Mr. Niall Lawless for his careful, professional and precise examination of this book.

**Wu Zhixin**

Feb. $22^{nd}$, 2020

# CONTENTS

**PREFACE**
**FOREWORD**

### CHAPTER I  GLOBAL CONSTRUCTION MARKET AND MARKETING

| | | |
|---|---|---|
| LESSON 1 | A CHANGING GLOBAL CONSTRUCTION MARKET | 002 |
| LESSON 2 | REGIONAL MARKET INVESTIGATIONS | 012 |
| LESSON 3 | ON AN INFRASTRUCTURE DEVELOPMENT CONFERENCE | 022 |
| LESSON 4 | SUBMITTING A LOI (LETTER OF INTEREST) | 030 |
| LESSON 5 | DRAFTING MOU (MEMORANDUM OF UNDERSTANDING) | 039 |

### CHAPTER II  PRE-CONTRACT ACTIVITIES OF BOT PROJECT

| | | |
|---|---|---|
| LESSON 6 | PROJECT INFORMATION COLLECTION & SITE INSPECTION | 048 |
| LESSON 7 | CONCEPTUAL DESIGN | 060 |
| LESSON 8 | FEASIBILITY STUDY & ENVIRONMENTAL IMPACT ASSESSMENT | 072 |
| LESSON 9 | SEEKING FINANCE FOR THE PROJECT | 087 |
| LESSON 10 | NEGOTIATIONS ON THE PROJECT CONCESSION AGREEMENT | 098 |

### CHAPTER III  CONTRACT IMPLEMENTATION OF BOT PROJECT

| | | |
|---|---|---|
| LESSON 11 | LOCAL REGISTRATION OF THE PROJECT COMPANY | 112 |
| LESSON 12 | LAND ACQUISITION FOR THE PROJECT | 121 |
| LESSON 13 | ARRANGING STONE QUARRIES FOR THE PROJECT | 130 |
| LESSON 14 | IMPORTING HEAVY MACHINERY FROM CHINA | 142 |
| LESSON 15 | LOCAL WORKERS RECRUITMENT | 152 |
| LESSON 16 | PROJECT SECURITY DEPLOYMENTS | 162 |
| LESSON 17 | FULFILLING SOCIAL RESPONSIBILITIES | 173 |
| LESSON 18 | WHOLE ROAD OPENING TO TRAFFIC | 183 |
| LESSON 19 | HIGHWAY OPERATION & MAINTENANCE | 193 |
| LESSON 20 | HIGHWAY TRANSFER TO THE LOCAL AUTHORITY | 204 |

# 目 录

序
前 言

## 第一章　全球工程市场与市场开拓

| | | |
|---|---|---|
| 第1课 | 变化中的全球建筑市场 | 008 |
| 第2课 | 区域市场调研 | 018 |
| 第3课 | 在基础设施开发国际大会上 | 027 |
| 第4课 | 呈送项目兴趣函 | 035 |
| 第5课 | 起草谅解备忘录 | 044 |

## 第二章　BOT项目签约前期工作

| | | |
|---|---|---|
| 第6课 | 项目信息搜集与现场踏勘 | 055 |
| 第7课 | 概念设计 | 067 |
| 第8课 | 可行性研究和环境影响评价 | 081 |
| 第9课 | 寻求项目融资 | 093 |
| 第10课 | 项目特许经营权协议谈判 | 105 |

## 第三章　BOT项目合同实施

| | | |
|---|---|---|
| 第11课 | 当地注册项目公司 | 117 |
| 第12课 | 项目征地 | 126 |
| 第13课 | 为项目安排采石场 | 137 |
| 第14课 | 从中国进口重型机械 | 148 |
| 第15课 | 招募当地工人 | 158 |
| 第16课 | 项目安防部署 | 168 |
| 第17课 | 履行社会责任 | 179 |
| 第18课 | 全线通车 | 189 |
| 第19课 | 高速路运营与养护 | 199 |
| 第20课 | 向地方当局移交高速路 | 211 |

# CHAPTER I  GLOBAL CONSTRUCTION MARKET AND MARKETING

A CHANGING GLOBAL CONSTRUCTION MARKET
REGIONAL MARKET INVESTIGATIONS
ON AN INFRASTRUCTURE DEVELOPMENT CONFERENCE
SUBMITTING A LOI ( LETTER OF INTEREST )
DRAFTING MOU ( MEMORANDUM OF UNDERSTANDING )

# 第一章  全球工程市场与市场开拓

变化中的全球建筑市场
区域市场调研
在基础设施开发国际大会上
呈送项目兴趣函
起草谅解备忘录

# CHAPTER I  GLOBAL CONSTRUCTION MARKET AND MARKETING

## LESSON 1  A CHANGING GLOBAL CONSTRUCTION MARKET

**Dialogue**

**Mr. Bai-President of International Contracting Company of Group M**

**Mr. Andersen-President of an International Infrastructure Investment Company**

**Mr. Anderson:** Mr. Bai, my old friend. Long time no see. How are you?

**Mr. Bai:** Mr. Anderson! I'm fine, how about you?

**Mr. Anderson:** Very well. I heard that you have been promoted to president of International Contracting Company of your group. Congratulations! I am not surprised given your outstanding achievement and performance in international construction.

**Mr. Bai:** Thanks for your compliment!

**Mr. Anderson:** China has been developing rapidly in past decades, and the market share of Chinese construction contractors in the global construction market is also growing fast. It is amazing!

**Mr. Bai:** It is hard to believe that our last meeting was about ten years ago. It is almost 20 years since China joined the WTO. Since then Chinese contractors have grown rapidly in the international construction market. My company has also made great achievement under the guidance of going-global strategy made by the Chinese government. However, to be honest, my company is facing certain bottlenecks and problems, which I'd like to share with you. Taking this opportunity, may I be honored to hear your foresight, and understand how you see future developments in the international engineering & contracting market?

**Mr. Anderson:** Well, yes, I have noticed some changes in the international engineering & contracting market, which I would be very happy to discuss with you. But why don't you describe your situation first?

**Mr. Bai:** Great! Our company's main business has been concentrated in underdeveloped countries in Asia, Africa, Central and Eastern Europe and Latin America. But encumbered by the fallout from the financial crisis in 2008 and European debt crisis in 2012, the economic activity of these countries has experienced a big down-turn and suffered deep slumps one after another. This has seriously affected the international trade and construction market. The underdeveloped countries that heavily rely on the export of natural resources for foreign exchange were struck heavily by the decline of crude oil and minerals prices. Accordingly, their fiscal revenue declined sharply and their construction budgets were cut dowm deeply. Sadly, some of our projects' payments were delayed severely. Recently we have noticed that new project opportunities generally require contractors to have the ability to provide finance and investment.

**Mr. Anderson:** I also noticed this trend. It seems these difficulties are not only encountered by Chinese contractors, but also by other contractors all over the world. I believe that among Asia, Africa, Central and Eastern Europe, and Latin America, the Asian economy is much better than the other regions comparatively.

**Mr. Bai:** Oh, for us the Middle East is also part of the Asia regions, but the Middle East is volatile, and in many countries the situation is very tense and unpredictable, even in the short-term. For example, the war in Syria has been going on for years, and the Israeli-Palestinian conflict is not resolving itself.

**Mr. Anderson:** Yes, but if you just consider the Central and Southeast Asian countries, and India, they seem to be resuming their economic momentum and showing great development potential. I believe their governments' ability to fund projects and make prompt payments.

**Mr. Bai:** Great, we share the same perspective. These countries are adjacent to China and they have always been our key markets. But you know, competition in these countries is becoming more intense.

**Mr. Anderson:** I agree with you. In my opinion, Africa is the most potential continent with its vast territory and rich resources. Most of the African countries are still at the primary stage of economic development. So they have a strong focus on basic infrastructure development and how to enhance the opportunity for their people to have a good livelihood.

**Mr. Bai:** Our company is working on many projects in Africa too, including some aid projects funded by Chinese government as well as more projects financed by Chinese banks.

**Mr. Anderson:** The Latin America market is growing fast too, but you need to pay close attention to the market risk.

**Mr. Bai:** Yes, we feel that there are complicated laws and because the labor unions are strong in this region, it constrains the contracting business badly.

**Mr. Anderson:** While the Central and Eastern Europe markets have been hit by Europe's sovereign debt crisis, economic uncertainty is rising and capital investment is falling sharply. In comparison with Asia and Africa, the construction markets there are relatively mature and you will find the criterias for market admittance, labor policy and technical standards are much stricter.

**Mr. Bai:** We also realized the challenges of these factors. Therefore we decided not to pursue many opportunities in this region.

**Mr. Anderson:** Each continent faces its own difficulties. For sure, the contraction of the world's economies has affected the international contracting industry a lot.

**Mr. Bai:** You are right! Due to the lower price of bulk commodities, many developing countries relying on natural resources have encountered tough circumstances. Because of the sharp reduction in capital investment budgets and the ability to provide reliable financial guarantees, F+EPC projects are less and less adopted, while the PPP, BOT construction projects are more and more common. In this new market environment, our company is trying to transit its business model to adapt to the current situation.

**Mr. Anderson:** The Chinese government was far-sighted in launching the Belt and Road Initiative. This has played a strong role in stimulating the economies of many countries, and created many opportunities in the international contracting and engineering market. It also led the establishment of Asian Infrastructure Investment Bank, to support infrastructure construction in developing countries. I truly admire this.

**Mr. Bai:** The initiative proposed by Chinese government does play an important role in promoting the international construction contracting industry. Our company works closely with the big policy banks such as China Export-Import Bank, China Development Bank and other state-owned commercial banks like Industrial and Commercial Bank of China, and Bank of China to assist foreign governments in financing and promoting appropriate infrastructure projects. At the same time, we also have good links with various funds, such as Silk Road Fund, China-Africa Development Fund and China-Africa Fund for Industrial Cooperation to implement investment projects, PPP and BOT projects.

**Mr. Anderson:** That's very inspiring to hear. As a matter of fact, the developed countries are also facing the problem of lack of funds for infrastructure reconstruction. I hope you can come to my country to investigate and conduct business there in PPP model. I can introduce you some of my good friends who might be very helpful to your business start-up.

**Mr. Bai:** Thank you very much, Mr. Anderson. I would be very glad to cooperate with you in the future, wherever in your country or other countries you recommend.

## Key-words & Expressions

| | |
|---|---|
| Global construction market | 全球建筑市场 |
| International engineering & contracting market | 国际工程承包市场 |
| Financial crisis | 金融危机 |
| Sovereign debts crisis | 主权债务危机 |
| Economic momentum | 经济势头 |
| OBOR (The Belt and Road Initiative) | "一带一路"倡议 |
| Capital investment | 基本建设投资 |
| F+EPC (Finance + Engineering-Procurement-Construction) | 融资加设计、采购、施工模式 |
| PPP (Public-Private Partnership) | 政府和社会资本合作模式 |
| BOT (Build-Operation-Transfer) | 建造-运营-移交模式 |
| Financial guarantee | 融资担保 |
| AIIB (Asian Infrastructure Investment Bank) | 亚洲基础设施投资银行 |
| China Export-Import Bank | 中国进出口银行 |
| China Development Bank | 中国国家开发银行 |
| Industrial and Commercial Bank of China | 中国工商银行 |
| Silk Road Fund | 丝路基金 |
| China-Africa Development Fund | 中非发展基金 |
| China-Africa Fund for Industrial Cooperation | 中非产能合作基金 |

# 第一章　全球工程市场与市场开拓

## 第1课　变化中的全球建筑市场

### 对话

**白先生 - M 集团国际承包公司总裁**

**Andersen 先生 - 某国际基础设施投资公司总裁**

**Anderson 先生**：白先生，我的老朋友，好久没见啦。你还好吗？

**白先生**：Anderson 先生！我很好啊，你呢？

**Anderson 先生**：我也很好。我听说你已经被提升为贵集团国际工程与承包公司总裁啦。恭喜啊！鉴于你在国际工程市场上的出色表现，我并不感到意外。

**白先生**：谢谢你的夸奖！

**Anderson 先生**：过去的几十年里中国一直在快速发展，中国承包商在全球工程市场所占的市场份额也在快速增长。这真是神奇啊！

**白先生**：很难相信自从我们上次见面以来十年已经过去了。中国加入世界贸易组织也有近20年的时间了。中国承包商在国际工程市场上快速成长。我公司在中国政府"走出去"战略的指引下也取得了巨大的成就。不过坦率地说，我愿意把我们公司面临的一些瓶颈和问题也告诉你。借此机会，我能否有幸聆听你的远见卓识，并了解你对未来国际工程承包市场前景的看法呢？

**Anderson 先生**：好啊，我也注意到国际工程承包市场的一些变化，很乐意跟你讨论。但是你为什么不先描述一下你的情况呢？

**白先生**：好极了！我们公司的业务集中在亚洲、非洲、中东欧以及拉丁美洲的欠发达国家。但受到2008年金融危机和2012年欧洲债务危机的拖累，这些国家的经济一落千丈、一蹶不振，严重影响到国际贸易和国际工程市场。由于原油和矿产价格的下跌，严重依赖资源出口换取外汇的欠发达国家受到沉重的打击，他们的财政收入乃至建设预算都大幅下降。很遗憾我们有几个项目的付款都遭到严重拖延。最近我们注意到，新项目机会一般都要求承包商具有一定的投资和融资能力。

**Anderson 先生**：我也注意到了这个趋势。这些困难似乎不仅是中国承包商所面临的，也是世界各地其他承包商所都面临的。我认为，在亚洲、非洲、中东欧和拉丁美洲国家中，亚洲国家经济形势相对好于其他地区。

**白先生**：哦，对我们来说中东地区也属于亚洲地区的一部分，但中东局势动荡，许多国家的形势极端紧张和不可预测。例如，叙利亚战争持续了多年，再加上巴以冲突并没有得到解决。

**Anderson 先生**：不错。但是如果仅仅考虑中亚、东南亚国家和印度，这些国家的经济势头正在复苏，显示出强劲的发展潜力。我相信他们政府有能力投资项目并及时付款。

**白先生**：太好了，我们俩观点一致。这些国家与中国毗邻，一直是我们的主要市场。但你知道，那里的竞争变得更加激烈了。

**Anderson 先生**：我同意你的观点。在我看来，非洲幅员辽阔、资源丰富，是最具潜力的大陆。大多数非洲国家仍处于经济发展的初级阶段。所以他们专注于基本的基础设施建设和增强民生保障。

**白先生**：我们公司在非洲也有很多项目，包括一些由中国政府援建的项目，以及更多由中国的银行提供融资的项目。

**Anderson 先生**：拉美市场也在快速增长，不过你要密切关注那里的市场风险。

**白先生**：是的，我们觉得这个地区有着复杂的法律，并且由于工会很强势，这都严重制约着工程承包业务。

**Anderson 先生**：中东欧市场受到欧洲主权债务危机的影响，那里的经济的不确定性上升，基本建设投资大幅下降。与亚洲和非洲相比，那里的建筑市场相对成熟，你会发现他们的市场准入、劳工政策和技术标准都要严格得多。

**白先生**：我们也注意到了这些挑战性因素，所以我们决定不在该地区寻求太多项目机会。

**Anderson 先生**：每个大洲都有各自的困难。当然，世界经济的紧缩已经对国际工程承包业产生了很大影响。

**白先生**：你是对的！由于大宗商品价格低迷，许多依赖自然资源的发展中国家面临着艰难的境地。由于基本建设投资和融资担保能力的大幅下降，采用 F+EPC 模式的项目越来越少，而采用 PPP、BOT 模式的建设项目则越来越多。在这一新的市场环境下，我公司正努力进行业务转型，以适应当前的形势。

**Anderson 先生：**中国政府以其远见卓识提出了"一带一路"倡议，为推动世界经济特别是为国际工程承包市场创造机会发挥了重要作用。中国还牵头创建了亚洲基础设施投资银行，支持发展中国家的基础设施建设，我对此十分钦佩。

**白先生：**中国政府提出的这一倡议对促进国际工程承包行业的发展具有重要作用。我公司与中国进出口银行、国家开发银行等政策性银行及中国工商银行、中国银行等国有商业银行都有密切的合作，协助外国政府融资，推动相关项目的落地。同时，我们还与丝路基金、中非发展基金、中非产能合作基金等各类基金有密切联系，来实施投资项目、PPP 项目和 BOT 项目。

**Anderson 先生：**这真是非常鼓舞人心啊。事实上，发达国家也面临着基础设施建设资金不足的问题。我希望你们也能来我的国家进行调研，并以 PPP 模式开展业务。我会把我的一些好朋友介绍给你，他们将对你们的业务初创有很大帮助。

**白先生：**非常感谢你，Anderson 先生。我很乐意将来与你合作，无论是在你的国家还是你推荐的其他国家。

## LESSON 2  REGIONAL MARKET INVESTIGATIONS

### Dialogue

**Mr. Bai-President of International Contracting Company of Group M**

**Mr. Huang-President of H Division, Vice President of International Contracting Company of Group M**

**Mr. Frederick-International Construction Market Consultant**

**Mr. Bai:** My friend, Mr. Anderson introduced me to a market expert who has been researching Continent H for decades. Mr. Huang, this is Mr. Frederick.

**Mr. Huang:** How do you do, Mr. Frederick.

**Mr. Frederick:** Nice to meet you. Mr. Bai told me that you are in charge of the construction and engineering business in Continent H.

What can I do for you, Mr. Huang?

**Mr. Huang:** I read Economic Herald recently and there was a very interesting article describing that new oil and gas resources have been found in Region O of Continent H. How do you feel this discovery will affect the construction contracting market in this region?

**Mr. Bai:** Two weeks ago, Mr. Anderson sent me an email saying that the political difficulties seemed to have been resolved and suggested me to grasp big opportunities in Region O. Mr. Frederick, your opinions regarding Region O will be very influential in guiding our company's decision. Can you tell me how you see the situation?

**Mr. Frederick:** All right, Mr. Bai. My consultancy firm has been following the situation of Region O for nearly ten years. Noticing the recent turn around in the region, my colleagues and I undertook a preliminary investigation on the relevant countries in Region O.

**Mr. Bai:** Great, are you willing to share the outline of your preliminary investigations right now?

**Mr. Frederick:** Traditionally, the main construction contracting market of Continent H is in the north, which is rich in oil and gas resources. Also the political environment there is relatively stable. As I know, your company has two projects underway in the north. Naturally, well-known contractors around the world gathered there, and the competition is relatively fierce. Contrary to the north, the south-Region O has not attracted much attention. The main reasons for this were the on-going conflict and the political instability. Affected by the politics, economic development was slow and even going backwards. There was little investment in infrastructure and people lived in poverty. In addition, this region was previously considered to be poor in natural resources. The few contractors who entered that area did not make profit and even suffered losses in the past, so there were no more contractors willing to enter.

**Mr. Bai:** You'd better focus on the latest situation.

**Mr. Frederick:** Well, in recent years, the political situation in Region O has changed a lot. Local people want peace, development and prosperity. The governments have launched a new round of economic development plans and adopted the "Look East" diplomatic and economic strategy, hoping to strengthen economic and trade cooperation with China.

**Mr. Huang:** Over the years, China has provided geological survey assistance free, and a number of valuable mineral resources have been discovered in the region. This provides a good foundation for economic development.

**Mr. Frederick:** Yes. Therefore, I totally agree with Mr. Anderson that Region O has a huge market potential. Before Region O attracts more companies, you should consider how to enter and explore this market expeditiously.

**Mr. Huang:** Yes, it is better to be the early bird.

**Mr. Bai:** After hearing your summary, I become more confident in making the decision to enter Region O, but there are seven countries in this region, A, B, C, D, E, F and G. Which country is the best to enter first?

**Mr. Frederick:** Our firm has considered the precedence order. After analysis, we believe that A is the country with best conditions. First of all, nearly 1/3 of the newly discovered oil and gas resources are in this country, the export of this oil and gas can quickly improve the country's finance situation and transform the country's fiscal revenue. secondly, A has the best geographical location, adjacent to the ocean with a natural harbor. Our third reason is that during the first half of this year, support rate for Party X, which stands for peaceful development, rose by 23% among the electorate, while the support rate for Party Y, which supports extremist forces fell by 29%. Therefore, Party X won the election by a wide margin. The new president of country A is dedicated to developing the economy of the country, try to introduce policies to attract talents from overseas, and encourage emigrant nationals living abroad to return home. Additionally, in order to attract foreign investment, a number of preferential policies have been put in place, especially the newly launched Law of Private Investment and PPP Act, aimed at attracting funds with international and private capital to invest in the country's infrastructure development. They planned to carry out a number of infrastructure projects related to the national economy and people's livelihood in PPP model.

**Mr. Huang:** Politically, sincere friendship has been built between Country A and China. You will recall the president of Country A visited China shortly after his inauguration. The leaders of the two countries confirmed their desire and plan on expanding capacity cooperation between the two sides.

**Mr. Frederick:** Meanwhile, other countries are still facing significant problems. Countries B and C could be classed as currently politically unstable, there are a lot of strong disturbances caused by the opposition parties. Few pollsters believe that the current government will survive the general election next year. The domestic security situation continues to worsen; and terrorist attacks have taken place in these countries. D and E are inland countries, the economies of which have stagnated for a long time. Although that is in some ways attractive and there are abundant mineral resources, they are lack of the ability to transport mineral resources abroad to earn foreign exchanges due to their poor infrastructure. Despite the political stability, the ruling party presents itself as quite conservative; there is no sign of it opening-up. Country F prefers to look to the West and has been unwilling to establish diplomatic relations with China. Accordingly, Chinese companies would not have a sound diplomatic foundation to undertake business, so we would recommend that country F should not be considered by your company right now. As to Country G, which is enduring sanctions imposed by Western countries, the very strict control of foreign exchange makes cross-border currency remittance almost impossible. In conclusion, I suggest that you should enter Country A first, and then take that as a business base for radiating to the adjacent countries.

**Mr. Huang:** Mr. Bai, I've just received an invitation to attend the International Conference on Infrastructure Development which will be held in Country A on the $5^{th}$ day of next month. I believe that will be a good opportunity for us to meet with people on the ground and to start to get involved.

**Mr. Bai:** Very good. I agree that it is appropriate to enter Country A. Mr. Frederick, please investigate and report formally to us regarding the legal framework and foreign investment policy of Country A. Mr. Huang, I want to task you with collecting specific projects information for Country A. Next month, I will lead our team to attend the International Conference on Infrastructure Development. Let's schedule some meetings with the local government and additionally we spend time investigating the local market further.

**Mr. Huang:** All right, I'll arrange the itinerary.

## Key-words & Expressions

| | |
|---|---|
| Economic Herald | 经济导报 |
| Preliminary investigation | 初步调查 |
| Fierce competition | 激烈竞争 |
| Political environment (Political situation) | 政局 |
| Political instability | 政局不稳定 |
| Extremist forces | 极端势力 |
| Terrorist attacks | 恐怖袭击 |
| Diplomatic and economic strategy | 外交和经济战略 |
| Economic and trade cooperation | 经贸合作 |
| Mineral resources | 矿产资源 |
| Market potential | 市场潜力 |
| Being the early bird | 当早起的鸟 |
| Precedence order | 优先顺序 |
| Pollsters | 民意调查者，民意测验专家 |
| Conservative | 保守的 |
| Opening-up | 开放 |
| Fiscal revenue | 财政收入 |
| Geographical location | 地理位置 |
| Emigrant nationals living abroad | 移居海外的侨民 |
| Cross-border currency remittance | 跨境汇款 |
| International conference | 国际会议 |
| Legal framework | 法律体制 |
| Specific project information | 具体的项目信息 |
| Itinerary | 行程 |

# 第 2 课　区域市场调研

## 对话

**白先生 - M 集团国际承包公司总裁**

**黄先生 - H 事业部总经理，M 集团国际承包公司副总裁**

**Frederick 先生 - 国际工程市场咨询师**

**白先生：** 我的朋友 Anderson 先生为我介绍了一位研究 H 洲数十年的市场专家。黄先生，过来认识一下 Frederick 先生。

**黄先生：** 您好，Frederick 先生。

**Frederick 先生：** 很高兴认识你。白先生告诉我你在负责 H 洲的建设和工程业务。黄先生，我能为你做点什么？

**黄先生：** 我最近在经济导报上看到一篇很有趣的文章，谈到在 H 洲的 O 地区发现了新的油气资源。你觉得这个发现会对这个地区的工程承包市场有什么影响呢？

**白先生**：两周之前，Anderson 给我发来电子邮件说那里的政治困局似乎已经解决，建议我抓住进入 O 地区的大好机会。Frederick 先生，您关于 O 地区的看法对我们公司的决策将是非常有影响力的。我能否听听您是怎么想的呀？

**Frederick 先生**：好的，白先生。我的咨询事务所关注 O 地区的局势已经近十年啦。注意到这个地区近期的转机，我和我的同事对 O 地区有关国家作了个初步调查。

**白先生**：太好了，你是否愿意现在就分享下你们初步调查的要点呢？

**Frederick 先生**：H 大洲传统的工程承包市场主要集中在北部，那里的油气资源丰富，政局也相对稳定。据我所知，你们公司也有两个项目正在北部地区实施。世界各地的著名承包商都聚集到那里，竞争自然就相对激烈。然而与北部地区相反，南部地区——O 地区就没有受到足够的重视。其背后的主要原因是多年前持续不断的冲突和政局的不稳定。受政治因素的影响，经济发展迟缓甚至倒退。基础设施投资很少，人民生活贫困。此外，这里先前还被视为资源贫乏的地区。就在几年之前，只有少数承包商进入该地区，结果未能获利，甚至是亏损，因此没有更多承包商愿意去那里。

**白先生**：你最好还是聚焦于最近的情况吧。

**Frederick 先生**：好的，近年来 O 地区的政治形势有了新的转机。当地人民向往和平、发展和繁荣。各国政府启动了新一轮经济发展计划，并采取了"向东看"的外交和经济战略，希望加强与中国的经贸合作。

**黄先生**：多年以来中国无偿援助的地质勘察在该地区发现了一批有价值的矿产资源，为其经济发展提供了良好的基础。

**Frederick 先生**：是的。因此，我完全赞同 Anderson 先生的观点，O 地区具有巨大的市场潜力。你们最好在 O 地区吸引更多公司之前考虑如何迅速进入并开拓这一市场。

**黄先生**：是的，我们最好是捷足先登啊。

**白先生**：听了你的总结，我对进入 O 地区的决定就更有信心了，不过这个地区有 7 个国家，A、B、C、D、E、F 和 G 国，我们应该首先进入哪个国家呢？

**Frederick 先生**：我们事务所已经考虑了优先顺序。根据我们的分析，可以相信 A 国是条件最好的一个。首先，新发现的油气资源中近三分之一是在这个国家，油气资源出口可以迅速转化为国家的财政收入；其次，A 国地理位置优越，毗邻大海，拥有天然良港；第三，今年上半年主张和平发展的 X 政党支持率上升了 23%，而支持极端主义势力的 Y 政党支持率则下跌了 29%。最终 X 政党以巨大优势赢得了大选。A 国的新总统致力于发展国家经济，努力出台吸引海外人才的政策，鼓励海外侨民回国。此外，为吸引外国投资，已经出台了一些优惠政策，尤其是新颁布的《私人投资法》和《政府和社会资本合作法案》，吸引国际和私人资本投资该国的基础设施建设。他们计划以 PPP 模式实施一批关系国计民生的基础设施项目。

**黄先生**：在政治上 A 国和中国十分友好，你应该记得 A 国总统就职后不久即访问了中国，两国领导人确认了双方扩大产能合作的意愿和计划。

**Frederick 先生**：与此同时，其他国家则仍面临严峻的问题。B 国、C 国目前政局不稳，经受着来自反对党很强的干扰。几乎没有民意测验专家相信现任政党能在明年的大选中获胜。国内安全形势继续恶化，两个国家都发生恐怖袭击事件。D 国和 E 国都是内陆国家，两国经济徘徊不前。虽然在某些方面有吸引力并且矿产资源丰富，但由于基础设施落后，苦于缺乏将矿产运到国外换取外汇的能力。尽管政局尚属稳定，但执政党偏于保守，没有开放的迹象。F 国较亲西方，尚未有意愿与中国建立外交关系。因此，中国企业的业务在那里没有良好的外交基础，所以我们建议贵公司不应该把 F 国考虑在内。至于受到西方国家制裁的 G 国，那里对外汇的控制非常严格，跨境汇款几乎没有可能。总之，我建议你们应先进入 A 国，作为辐射周边国家的业务基地。

**黄先生**：白先生，我刚收到一张基础设施开发国际会议的邀请函，下月 5 日将在 A 国举行。我相信这将是我们与当地人民见面并开始介入其中的一个好机会。

**白先生**：很好。进入 A 国是恰当的，我同意。Frederick 先生，请正式对 A 国法律体制和外商投资政策进行调研并向我们汇报。黄先生，我给你一个任务去搜集 A 国的具体项目信息。下个月，我将带领团队去参加基础设施开发国际会议。我们与当地政府会安排一些会议，并进一步考察当地市场。

**黄先生**：好的，我来安排行程。

# LESSON 3  ON AN INFRASTRUCTURE DEVELOPMENT CONFERENCE

## Dialogue

**Mr. Bai-President of International Contracting Company of Group M**

**Mr. Fernando-Country A Minister, Ministry of Infrastructure Development**

**Mr. Bai:** Good morning, honorable minister. I am tremendously inspired by the report you outlined in your conference keynote presentation. It is my great honor to meet you. My name is Yu Bai, I am President of International Contracting Company of Group M in China. This is my business card.

**Mr. Fernando:** Nice meeting you, Mr. Bai.

**Mr. Bai:** Thanks, minister. Your keynote speech had many wonderful components. You presented not only the long term vision for your country, but you complemented that with a long-term development plan to make your vision real. Based on what we have seen so far, I think that your country is on the road to prosperity under the leadership of the government and you. I understand that you want me to tell you more about my company. Group M is one of the world's top five hundred companies and our company is also ranked in the top 30 among ENR's ranking of the 250 top international contractors. We undertake contracting and engineering activities in all the populated continents. Our company undertakes all kinds of infrastructure projects, including roads, railways, bridges, water supply, power, housing and so on. Accordingly, I believe our company has the complete ability to make a great contribution to the infrastructure development in your country. We hope to have the opportunity to serve your people under the framework of your development plan.

**Mr. Fernando:** Mr. Bai, I'm glad to meet you personally. Group M and your company are well-known and have a good reputation in global investment and contracting circles, with which I am very familiar. I heard you successfully completed the highway project in Country R of northern Continent H. We know that poor infrastructure is hindering our economic development. In order to revitalize the economy of our country, we have to improve our infrastructure first. We need and welcome superior international contracting companies like yours to take part in our infrastructure development.

**Mr. Bai:** Respected minister, thank you very much for these comments, they are greatly appreciated. Should we have the chance, we will be committed to accomplishing any tasks entrusted to us by your country. According to the experience of China's economic taking-off, we have a popular pet phrase "if you want to get rich, build roads first". I believe it also works in your country.

**Mr. Fernando:** Yes, I agree with you. The Chinese phrase is absolutely right. Therefore, one of the first initiatives we are planning is to build a 450 km West-east Highway replacing the old R1 Road to connect our biggest port, the capital and the border with Country D. This project is our number one priority and I would like to know whether you are interested in becoming involved with it?

**Mr. Bai:** Yes, of course, I am very interested! I also noticed in the report you presented that railway is also one of your prior projects, which we are very interested in as well.

**Mr. Fernando:** Railway is critical for the export of our mineral resources. At present we also need to upgrade our railway system urgently. I am glad that you are interested in railway projects as well. I would emphasize that another priority area for us is to utilize our abundant water resources for power generation and crops irrigation.

**Mr. Bai:** These projects are all within the competence and strengths of our company.

**Mr. Fernando:** As I mentioned in my report, all the infrastructure projects are planned to be implemented using the BOT model. Are you capable of undertaking these infrastructure projects using the BOT model?

**Mr. Bai:** Yes, some of our projects have already been successfully performed on a BOT basis. We have the capability and experience to perform BOT projects.

**Mr. Fernando:** Great!

**Mr. Bai:** For the BOT projects, I would like to know what kind of preferential policies the contractors may enjoy.

**Mr. Fernando:** We have issued the Private Investment Law and the PPP Act, these stipulate the detailed provisions for BOT and PPP projects offering land acquisition privileges and big tax concessions in both the construction stage and operation stage. I recommend that you refer to and study these laws for detailed preferential policies.

**Mr. Bai:** Many thanks for meeting us today and giving us time from your busy schedule. Let me say it again, your detailed introduction and approach inspires me a lot. Please may I ask how we can get more detailed relevant information concerning the above projects? Our next step would be to make a study on these projects, so that we can make some proposals as to the best way forward.

**Mr. Fernando:** You can contact my secretary-Alice, for the details of the project information.

## Key-words & Expressions

| | |
|---|---|
| Honorable minister | 尊敬的部长先生 |
| Keynote speech | 主题演讲 |
| Long-term development plan | 长期发展规划 |
| Global top five hundred companies | 世界500强企业 |
| ENR (Engineering News Report) | 工程新闻记录 |
| World's investment and contracting circle | 世界投资与承包界 |
| Bottleneck | 瓶颈 |
| Revitalize the economy | 振兴经济 |
| Economic taking-off | 经济起飞 |

| | |
|---|---|
| Prior project | 优先项目 |
| Pet phrase ( catch phrase ) | 口头禅 |
| If you want to get rich, build road first | 要致富先修路 |
| Abundant water resources | 丰富的水力资源 |
| Power generation | 发电 |
| Crops irrigation | 农作物灌溉 |
| Preferential policies | 优惠政策 |
| Private Investment Law | 私人投资法 |
| PPP Act | 政府和社会资本合作法案 |
| Land acquisition privilege | 征地优惠 |
| Tax concessions | 税收减免 |

# 第 3 课　在基础设施开发国际大会上

## 对话

**白先生 - M 集团国际承包公司总裁**

**Fernando 先生 - A 国基础设施开发建设部部长**

**白先生：**早上好，尊敬的部长先生。您刚才所作的主题演讲给了我极大的鼓舞。能与您见面真是非常荣幸。我叫白宇，是中国 M 集团国际承包公司总裁。这是我的名片。

**Fernando 先生：**很高兴认识你，白先生。

**白先生：**谢谢部长。您的主题演讲有很多精彩的部分。您不仅展示了你们国家的长远眼光，而且还为此提出一个长期发展规划。据我们目前所见，我认为贵国将在政府和您的领导下走上繁荣昌盛的大道。我知道您想让我告诉您更多关于我公司的情况。M 集团是世界 500 强企业之一，我们公司也名列 ENR 全球 250 家顶级国际承包商的前 30 位。我们的工程承包业务遍及各大洲，承接包括公路、铁路、桥梁、供水、电力和住房等各类基础设施项目。因此，我相信我们公司完全有能力为贵国的基础设施建设作出巨大贡献。我们希望有机会在你们的发展计划框架下为贵国人民服务。

**Fernando 先生：**白先生，很高兴见到你本人。M 集团和贵公司在世界投资和承包界享誉盛名，对此我耳熟能详。我听说你们在 H 洲北部的 R 国高速公路项目中取得了成功。我们知道基础设施落后已经严重阻碍了我们这个国家的经济发展。为了振兴我国经济，首先必须改善我们的基础设施。我们需要并且欢迎像你们这样的国际优秀承包公司来参与我们的基础设施建设。

**白先生：**尊敬的部长先生，谢谢您的评价，非常感激。如有机会，我们将坚定地尽我们的最大努力来完成贵国委托的任务。根据中国经济腾飞的经验，我们有一个流行的口头禅"要致富、先修路"。我相信在你们国家也是如此。

**Fernando 先生：**是啊，我同意你所说的。中国的这个口头禅说得太对了。因此，我们计划的首批举措之一是修建一条 450 公里的东西高速公路取代原有的 R1 公路，把我们最大的港口、首都以及与 D 国的边境连在一起。这是我们最优先的项目，我想知道你对此是否有兴趣？

**白先生：**是的，我当然很感兴趣！我注意到在您的报告中，铁路也是你们优先项目之一，我们也很感兴趣。

**Fernando 先生：**铁路对我们的矿产资源出口至关重要。当前我们急需对我们的铁路系统进行升级。我很高兴你对这个项目也感兴趣。另一个优先项目是利用我们丰富的水力资源来发电和灌溉农作物。

**白先生：**这些项目都是我公司的强项。

**Fernando 先生：**正如我在报告中提到的，所有基础设施项目都计划采用 BOT 模式。你们有能力按 BOT 模式实施这些项目吗？

**白先生：**是的，我们有一些项目已经按 BOT 模式成功实施了。我们有能力和经验执行好 BOT 项目。

**Fernando 先生：**很好！

**白先生：**关于 BOT 项目，我想知道承包商可以享受哪些优惠政策呢。

**Fernando 先生：**我们颁布了《私人投资法》和《政府与社会资本合作法案》，对 BOT 和 PPP 项目在建设阶段及运营阶段给予征地优惠和大额税收减免优惠作了具体规定。我建议你可以参阅这些法规了解详细的优惠政策。

**白先生：**非常感谢您在百忙之中与我们见面。让我再表达一次，您给我们作了如此周详的介绍，真让我茅塞顿开。请问我怎么才能够获得上述项目的相关资料？我们下一步将对这些项目进行研究，以便能制定一些以最佳方式推进项目的建议书。

**Fernando 先生：**你可以联系我的秘书 Alice 以取得这些项目的详细资料。

# LESSON 4  SUBMITTING A LOI (LETTER OF INTEREST)

## Dialogue 1

**Mr. Zhang-Manager of Marketing Department of International Contracting Company**

**Ms. Alice-Secretary of Minister Fernando**

**Mr. Zhang:** Good morning, Ms. Alice.

**Ms. Alice:** Good morning.

**Mr. Zhang:** I'm Zhang Ke, manager of the Marketing Department of International Contracting Company of Group M, Here is my business card. Yesterday, the president of our company Mr. Bai met with minister Fernando and discussed infrastructure projects in your country. We expressed our wish to participate in these projects, and the minister extended welcome to us and promised to provide relevant project information. He said we could obtain relevant information from you like master plans, topographic maps describing the West-east Highway Project, the National Railway Upgrading Project and Hydropower Station Project. May I have copies of the aforesaid information?

**Ms. Alice:** Yes, the minister instructed me yesterday to provide you with relevant information. For the West-east Highway Project, we have the master plan, 1 : 10000 topographic map and preliminary technical specifications. For the Railway Upgrading Project, we have proposed route plans for the high-speed railway network and a detailed map of the current rail network. For the Hydropower Station Project, we have the project preliminary design setting out the capacity requirements and 1 : 10000 topographic maps.

**Mr. Zhang:** Great, may I make a copy now?

**Ms. Alice:** No, not today. First of all, you need to submit a Letter of Interest; I can only provide you the relevant information after receiving your LOI and following that formal approval by the minister to give you the relevant information.

**Mr. Zhang:** Ok, so no problem with that. May I ask do you have any detailed requirements for the LOI; is there a specific format we should follow?

**Ms. Alice:** We have no specific requirements for LOI, but I recommend that you start by expressing your appreciation to the honorable minister and then set out what projects you are interested in, where you have acquired the project information. You should also provide information as to why your company is the best company to undertake these projects. If you have examples of similar projects undertaken in other countries, you should mention that.

**Mr. Zhang**: Ok, I understand. As to the initial greeting in the LOI, may I start as "Dear honorable minister, we appreciate and value the time you gave to us at the Infrastructure Development Conference. We hereby express our special thanks to you for your kind introduction outlining the West-east Highway Project, the National Railway Upgrading Project and the Hydropower Station Project. We have the experience and resources to undertake these important projects, and we are very interested in doing so."

**Ms. Alice**: Good, then you need to introduce your company and show your capability in doing these kinds of projects.

**Mr. Zhang**: We have successfully undertaken many similar projects around the world. I will outline our portfolio of achievements, and I trust you will recognize our company as well-qualified to work for Country A.

**Ms. Alice**: Sure, and you also need to clarify which model you plan to adopt for implementing these projects.

**Mr. Zhang**: Ok, I will remember this.

**Ms. Alice**: Then in the LOI you should list the information you need. You should also explain what resources you envisage bringing to this country; this is very important. Finally, the LOI should be signed by the president of your company, and be stamped with your company's seal.

**Mr. Zhang**: Oh, I am sorry. What do you mean by resources we might bring to the country? Do you mean the materials or machines that we might bring into this country?

**Ms. Alice:** No, no. I mean the benefits your company might bring to our country with the unique advantages of your company should you be awarded the contracts regarding the projects. For example, access to preferential finance, special technologies, quick delivery of the projects or more job opportunities for the local residents.

**Mr. Zhang:** I understand now. In this case, we shall prepare LOI expeditiously and submit our LOI as soon as possible. Thanks for your detailed instruction. Bye!

**Ms. Alice:** You are welcome, bye!

### Dialogue 2

**Mr. Zhang:** Ms. Alice, we very much appreciate the guidance you gave us when we last met. We have prepared our LOI. Please check and receive.

**Ms. Alice:** Wonderful! I believe that the minister will be satisfied after reading this.

**Mr. Zhang:** I'm glad to get your appreciation. We hope to contribute on your beautiful country. As a record of your receiving, I need your signature on this paper. Please sign here!

**Ms. Alice:** Ok, I will hand your LOI over to the minister as soon as possible. Please come back after 10 working days. If the Minister has approved, you may take the documents away.

**Mr. Zhang:** I understand. Thanks, and see you next time!

## Key-words & Expressions

| | |
|---|---|
| LOI (Letter of Interest) | 兴趣函 |
| Extend welcome to… | 对……表示欢迎 |
| Master plan | 总体规划 |
| Topographic map | 地形图 |
| West-East Highway Project | 东西高速公路项目 |
| National Railway Upgrading Project | 国家铁路升级改造项目 |
| Hydropower Station Project | 水电站项目 |
| Preliminary design | 初步设计 |
| Specific requirements | 特殊要求 |
| Preferential finance | 优惠融资 |
| Special technology | 专门技术 |
| Quick delivery | 快速交付 |

# 第 4 课　呈送项目兴趣函

## 对话 1

**张先生 - 国际承包公司市场部经理**
**Alice 小姐 - Fernando 部长的秘书**

**张先生**：Alice 小姐早上好。

**Alice 小姐**：早上好。

**张先生**：我是张珂，M 集团国际承包公司的市场部经理，这是我的名片。昨天，我们公司的总裁白先生拜见了部长 Fernando 先生并讨论了贵国的基础设施项目。我们表达了参与这些项目的愿望。部长对我们表示欢迎，并承诺提供相关的项目信息。他说我们可以从你那里取得描述东西高速公路、国家铁路升级改造、水电站等项目的总体规划、地形图等资料。我可以拿到上述资料的复印件吗？

**Alice 小姐**：可以的，昨天部长已经指示我向你们提供相关信息。对于东西高速公路项目，我们有总体规划、1：10000地形图和初步技术规范；铁路升级改造项目，我们有高速铁路网的建议规划和现有铁路网的详细线路图；水电站项目，我们有给定功率要求的项目初步设计和1：10000地形图。

**张先生**：太好了，我现在可以拿一份复印件吗？

**Alice 小姐**：不行，今天还不行。首先，你们需要提交一份兴趣函；我需要收到你们的兴趣函并取得部长正式批准后才能为你们提供相关信息。

**张先生**：好的，没问题。对兴趣函你们有什么具体要求吗，有没有我们需遵循的特定格式？

**Alice 小姐**：对兴趣函我们并没有什么特别的要求，不过我建议你们需要对尊敬的部长表达你们的谢意，并具体说明你们对哪些项目感兴趣，还有你们是从哪里得到那些项目信息的。你们还应该提供信息以证明为什么你们公司是执行这些项目最佳的公司。如果你们有在其他国家从事类似项目的案例，你们应该在函中提及。

**张先生**：好的，我明白了。关于意向书的第一句话，开头我可以这样写吗，"尊敬的部长先生，我们非常感谢您在基础设施开发建设大会上让我们占用您的宝贵时间。您为我们概要地描述了东西高速公路项目、国家铁路升级改造项目以及水电站项目，在此我们对您的介绍表示由衷的感谢。我们有经验和资源来承担这些重要的项目，我们对这些项目都非常感兴趣。"

**Alice 先生**：很好，接着你需要介绍你们自己的公司并展示你们实施这类项目的能力。

**张先生**：我们在世界各地做过许多类似的项目。我会把我们的业绩列在兴趣函里，并且我相信你们一定会认识到我们公司完全够格为 A 国服务的。

**Alice 小姐**：好的，你还需要阐明你们打算以何种模式来做这些项目。

**张先生**：好的，我会记住的。

**Alice 小姐**：然后，你要在函里列出你们所需的信息。还有一点非常重要，你们最好解释一下你们打算为这个国家带来些什么资源。最后，需要你们总裁的签字并盖上你们公司的印章。

**张先生**：哦，对不起。你说的我们带资源到这个国家是什么意思？你指的是我们会带入这个国家的材料和机器吗？

**Alice 小姐**：不，不是的。我的意思是，如果贵公司被授予这些项目的有关合同，以贵公司特有的优势你们会为我们国家带来什么益处，比如优惠融资、特种技术、项目快速交付以及为当地居民提供更多就业岗位。

**张先生**：这回我明白了。这样，我们会认真准备并尽快提交我们的兴趣函。谢谢你周详的指导。再见！

**Alice 小姐**：不客气，再见！

## 对话 2

**张先生**：Alice 小姐，非常感谢上次见面您给我们的指导，我们已经准备好了兴趣函。请你查收。

**Alice 小姐**：太好了！我相信部长读了这封函件一定会满意的。

**张先生：**得到你的夸奖我很高兴。我们希望能为你们美丽的国家做出贡献。作为你收到函件的一个记录，我需要你在这张纸上签字。请签在这里！

**Alice 小姐：**好的，我会尽快把这封函件呈给部长。请在十个工作日后再来。如果部长批准了，你们就可以把那些文件拿走。

**张先生：**我明白。谢谢，下次见！

# LESSON 5  DRAFTING MOU (MEMORANDUM OF UNDERSTANDING)

## Dialogue

**Mr. Bai-President of International Contracting Company of Group M**

**Mr. Fernando-Minister, Ministry of Infrastructure Development**

**Mr. Fernando:** I am so glad to see your strong desire and sincerity of participating in and serving my country's infrastructure development needs from your Letter of Interest. I believe you have received all the relevant project documents from Ms. Alice.

**Mr. Bai:** Yes, we have received all the documents. Based on the documents you provided we have undertaken a preliminary study. Our conclusion is that these projects can be implemented on BOT basis. We plan to have a series of field investigations and start with necessary groundwork for the projects. Your strong support is urgently needed during our further investigation and preliminary planning.

**Mr. Fernando:** No problem. I appreciate your proactive approach; it demonstrates your commitment to these projects. The Ministry of Infrastructure Development will provide the assistance and support necessary for your investigations.

**Mr. Bai:** Thanks for your trust and support, honorable minister. Will it be possible to prepare and sign a MOU for the preparatory work of these projects to clarify the obligation of both parties and attach an action list of work activities to be undertaken leading to the signing of a formal contract document? This would support both parties and provide certainty as to the way forward.

**Mr. Fernando:** I fully agree with you. But we ask that the MOU will only cover the highway project first. This is because the highway project is of top strategic significance to our country, it ranks first among the overall infrastructure development initiatives. The others would be further arranged latter.

**Mr. Bai:** OK, we will focus on the highway project first in accordance with your objectives. In order to drive the highway project forward, our company will conduct the required preparatory work, including research on the regional economic situation and the economic development forecasts. We will document the existing traffic flow based on our surveys and with your help document a long-term traffic forecast. We want to undertake a topographic survey along the optional routes and geological survey at key sections. These will help us to decide the best highway route considering both economic and environmental factors. Once we have compiled the feasibility study and undertaken preliminary design, we can use this information to determine the financing structure and move forward to obtain support from financial institutions. Our dedicated highway project team will work best if we have a special person from the ministry assigned to the team. He can assist us and guide us by contacting relevant ministries and local governments along the route as well as providing us the necessary technical, business, legal and tax information, etc.

**Mr. Fernando:** Your suggestion is very constructive and well received. We will arrange for Mr. Harold, director of Road Department from the ministry to assist you in every aspect. In the meantime, please proceed with the required work as quickly as possible. My ministry would expect the concession agreement to be signed within eight months. Please start detailed plan according to this timetable.

**Mr. Bai:** Oh, minister, I think it is unrealistic to undertake the work required including investigation, survey, design, feasibility study and putting the financing arrangement in eight months. It usually takes at least one year. As the philosophy of our company, the work quality must be put in the first place any time.

**Mr. Fernando:** I agree that the quality of work is most critical. Ok, please draw up a working plan for the preparatory work and make sure that it includes all the assumptions you have made. I would like to have that within three days, is that practical?

**Mr. Bai:** Yes, it is. Thank you for your understanding, minister, I have another request. Since there is a lot of work in need of the cooperation and coordination by the ministry as well as the support from the local governments, would you please appoint an official from the ministry to help us in preparing the plan? Your official can help us to ensure that the plan is rational and practical.

**Mr. Fernando:** Don't worry, Mr. Harold will help you with the plan and I suggest the preparatory work plan is attached to the MOU.

**Mr. Bai:** Thanks, minister. Bearing in mind that the preparatory work of such a project requires a lot of resources, I hope to add an exclusivity clause in the MOU.

**Mr. Fernando:** Well, I believe in your ability, but if you fail to finish preparatory work on time or the results are not satisfactory, we reserve the right to choose another contractor.

**Mr. Bai:** You can rest assured that we will finish the tasks at hand on time with good quality.

**Mr. Fernando:** Good. Then please draw up a MOU according to our discussions.

**Mr. Bai:** Ok, minister. We will submit the draft MOU for your review within three days attached with the preparatory work plan.

**Mr. Fernando:** It has been a very productive meeting! Mr. Bai, I look forward to seeing you next time.

## Key-words & Expressions

| | |
|---|---|
| MOU (Memorandum of Understanding) | 谅解备忘录 |
| Preparatory work | 准备工作 |
| Action list | 行动清单 |
| Of top strategic significance | 具有顶级战略重要性 |
| Regional economic situation | 区域经济形势 |
| Economic development forecast | 经济发展预测 |
| Existing traffic flow | 现有交通流量 |

| | |
|---|---|
| Long-term traffic forecast | 远期交通预测 |
| Topographic survey | 地形测量 |
| Optional routes | 备选线路 |
| Geological survey | 地质勘察 |
| Highway route | 高速公路的线路 |
| Feasibility study | 可行性研究 |
| Preliminary design | 初步设计 |
| Financing structure | 融资结构 |
| Financial institution | 金融机构 |
| Unrealistic | 不切合实际的 |
| Financing arrangement | 融资安排 |
| Philosophy of a company | 公司理念 |
| Exclusivity clause | 排他性条款 |
| Rest assured | 请放心，确信无疑 |
| Productive meeting | 富有成效的会议 |

## 第 5 课　起草谅解备忘录

### 对话

**白先生 - M 集团国际承包公司总裁**

**Fernando 先生 - 基础设施开发建设部部长**

**Fernando 先生：**我很高兴从你的来函里看到了你们为这个国家基础设施服务的强烈愿望和诚意。我相信你们已经从 Alice 小姐那里获得了有关项目的所有文件。

**白先生：**是的，我们已经收到了所有文件。我们已经对相关文件进行了初步研究。我们得出的结论是这些项目可以按 BOT 模式加以实施。我们计划进行一系列实地调查，为项目作必要的基础工作。我们进一步的调查和初步规划期间，迫切需要得到您的大力支持。

**Fernando 先生：**没问题。我欣赏你们积极主动的作风，这显示了你们对项目的承诺。基础设施开发建设部将为你们的调查提供有效的协助和必要的支持。

**白先生**：谢谢您的信任和支持，尊敬的部长先生。请问是否有可能在签订合同之前，我们就这些项目的筹备工作签署一份谅解备忘录以明确双方的义务，并附上一份到正式合同签署之前要开展的工作的行动清单？这将有助于双方切实推进项目。

**Fernando 先生**：我完全同意你的意见。但我们要求谅解备忘录首先只涵盖高速公路项目，因为该项目对我国具有顶级战略重要性，在基础设施建设中居于首位。其余项目将在稍后作进一步的安排。

**白先生**：好的，我们会按您的目标先把重点放在高速公路项目上。为了推进高速公路项目，我公司将进行必要的前期准备工作，包括区域经济形势研究和经济发展预测。我们也将根据我们的调查记录现有交通流量，并在你们的协助下进行远期交通预测。我们将在备选路线的沿线进行地形测量和关键路段的地质调查。这些将帮助我们在同时考量经济与环境因素的基础上确定高速公路的最佳线路。一旦我们完成编制可行性研究报告和初步设计，我们就可以利用这些信息来商定融资结构并获取金融机构的支持。如果贵部派出一名专人到我们团队来就最好了，他可以指导并协助我们联系沿线的相关部委和地方政府，提供必要的技术、商务、法律及税务等信息。

**Fernando 先生**：你的建议很好很有建设性。我们会安排这个部的道路司司长 Harold 先生从各个方面协助你们。同时，请尽快开展相关工作。我部希望在八个月内签订特许经营协议。请按这个时间表制定一份详细的计划。

**白先生**：哦，部长，我认为在八个月内完成包括调研、勘测、设计、可行性研究和融资安排等所有工作是不切合实际的。那通常至少需要一年的时间。作为我们公司的理念，任何时候都要把工作质量放在第一位。

**Fernando 先生**：我赞成工作质量是最关键的。好吧，请制定一份准备工作计划，并确保包含你所做的所有假设。我想在三天之内拿到这份计划，可以吗？

**白先生**：可以。谢谢您的理解，部长。我还有一个请求。由于许多工作需要贵部的配合和协调，还需要地方政府的支持，您能否从贵部任命一名官员来帮助我们起草计划呢？贵方官员可以在确保计划的合理性和落地性方面给我们很多帮助。

**Fernando 先生**：不用担心，Harold 先生会帮助你们编制计划的。我建议把准备工作计划附在谅解备忘录里。

**白先生**：谢谢部长。另外，请理解这样一个项目的准备工作需要大量的投入，我希望在谅解备忘录里增加一个排他性条款。

**Fernando 先生**：嗯，我相信你们的能力，但是如果你们不能按时完成准备工作或者结果不能令人满意，我们有权选择其他承包商。

**白先生**：您可以放心，我们会高质量地按时完成任务的。

**Fernando 先生**：好。那就请根据我们今天的讨论起草一份谅解备忘录吧。

**白先生**：好的，部长。我们会在三天内将谅解备忘录附上准备工作计划一起提交您审阅。

**Fernando 先生**：好一个富有成效的会议啊！白先生，期待下次见面。

# CHAPTER II  PRE-CONTRACT ACTIVITIES OF BOT PROJECT

PROJECT INFORMATION COLLECTION & SITE INSPECTION
CONCEPTUAL DESIGN
FEASIBILITY STUDY & ENVIRONMENTAL IMPACT ASSESSMENT
SEEKING FINANCE FOR THE PROJECT
NEGOTIATIONS ON THE PROJECT CONCESSION AGREEMENT

# 第二章  BOT 项目签约前期工作

项目信息搜集与现场踏勘
概念设计
可行性研究和环境影响评估
寻求项目融资
项目特许经营权协议谈判

# CHAPTER II  PRE-CONTRACT ACTIVITIES OF BOT PROJECT

## LESSON 6  PROJECT INFORMATION COLLECTION & SITE INSPECTION

**Dialogue 1**

**Mr. Li**-Manager of Engineering Department of International Contracting Company of Group M

**Mr. Harold**-Director of Road Department of Ministry of Infrastructure Development

**Mr. Li:** Good morning, Mr. Harold! Nice to see you again!

**Mr. Harold:** Good morning, Mr. Li! I am waiting for you to arrange relevant issues concerning the site investigation.

**Mr. Li:** You help us every time we need it. Thank you, Mr. Harold. Yesterday the minister and our president signed a MOU for the West-east Highway Project. The schedule that's been agreed is demanding, so we need to start working right now.

**Mr. Harold:** Yes, Mr. Li. But don't worry, I've got the minister's instruction yesterday and I am here to help you. I have informed municipal governments along the way already; they will also accompany us and make every effort to facilitate your investigation. And I will travel along the highway route together with your team. We need to prepare well before we commence more detailed site investigations. How many people from your team will be with me?

**Mr. Li:** There are four of us. I am the team leader and our team includes a design engineer, a surveyor and an estimator.

**Mr. Harold:** I'll notify the officials along the route so that they can arrange accommodation for you, but the transportation needs to be arranged by yourself.

**Mr. Li:** No problem. I will arrange a jeep available for the journey. It would be helpful if you could recommend me an experienced local driver who knows the terrain and is a veteran with this route. Such a person could help us to avoid difficulties along the way.

**Mr. Harold:** Of course, you can count on me. A friend of mine used to drive for our ministry helping out with highway network inspections. I will call him after this meeting, and he will contact you this afternoon to discuss the arrangements and what you want.

**Mr. Li:** That will be great. When shall we start off then? Would tomorrow be possible for you?

**Mr. Harold:** Not tomorrow. I have an important meeting tomorrow. I think we can start off the day after tomorrow. We are expected to traverse the entire 450km route so we must make full preparations.

**Mr. Li:** You are absolutely right. We've made a check list of the preparatory items for the site inspection. You see, there are two items we expect will be brought along by you, i.e. the topographic map and the highway network master plan.

**Mr. Harold:** I have prepared them already. I'll remember to bring them with me.

**Mr. Li:** We will load the RTK, GPS equipment, umbrellas for field survey and necessary medicines on the jeep in advance. Do you think we need to bring anything else?

**Mr. Harold:** That's so considerate of you.

**Mr. Li:** I'll pick you up at your ministry office building 8:00 a.m. the day after tomorrow.

**Mr. Harold:** Deal, see you then, and do remember to bring your passports with you.

## Dialogue 2

**Mr. Li-Manager of Engineering Department of International Contracting Company of Group M**

**Mr. Song-Road Designer of International Contracting Company of Group M**

**Mr. Zhong-Estimator of International Contracting Company of Group M**

**Mr. Harold-Director of Road Department of Ministry of Infrastructure Development**

**Mr. Jonathan-Local governor**

**Mr. Jonathan:** We have been looking over the east section of the route. Do you have any questions?

**Mr. Song:** I do have one question. According to the original highway network master plan and drawings, the design speed of the highway is indicated as 120 kilometers per hour. However, it seems to me that the route designed is not consistent with this speed. The gradients are too steep, and the curvature of the road is sharp in many places. This means the planned route is not the optimal one, for sure it will require huge earth works. In addition, I have noticed there are low-lying areas and wetlands in the path of the road, so the roadbed may need special treatment. I suggest special geological survey teams are dispatched to further investigate these areas.

**Mr. Harold:** The original master plan was made decades ago by a European company. The terrain has changed a lot comparing to that time, so it may not reflect the current situation.

**Mr. Jonathan:** Mr. Harold is right. It rains heavily here during the rainy season and this has changed the landform. In recent years, heavy rains have caused floods damaging crops and even destroyed bridges and the existing road.

**Mr. Song:** Mr. Harold, may I ask where I can get the precipitation records and rainstorm intensity formula of this area?

**Mr. Harold:** The meteorological department in the capital keeps all the data. After our return to the capital, we can buy the data from them.

**Mr. Jonathan:** Excuse me, I hope the new highway is planned to pass through City T which is a newly developed city in our province. Increasingly, there are plenty of high-valued agricultural products from the region pooled there and they need to be exported abroad.

**Mr. Song:** Let me take a look at the map. Ah, here it is. Detour to City T can just properly avoid the problem of steep gradients slope and sharp highway curvature in this area.

**Mr. Jonathan:** Oh, that's really good news!

**Mr. Li:** I have a question about the water sources. Road construction consumes a lot of water. Are there any suitable water sources nearby?

**Mr. Jonathan:** River R is about 20 km away from this section of road.

**Mr. Li:** How about the water flow rate and the water quality of River R? Is it a seasonal river?

**Mr. Jonathan:** Oh, don't worry. River R is one of the major rivers in our country and it has a high water flow during all seasons. The water volume should be sufficient for the construction.

**Mr. Li:** Good! We'll make further survey on it. How about a power supply for construction?

**Mr. Jonathan:** Our province has been facing serious power shortage for many years. I can do nothing to assist you with your power needs. You can only produce power for construction using diesel generators. The national oil company will be able to deliver diesel fuel to the local site.

**Mr. Li:** Are asphalt and aggregates available locally? If so, do you know what the prices are?

**Mr. Harold:** There is no asphalt plant in our country yet. Asphalt needs to be imported from abroad. There are many stone quarries in the mountainous area about 100 km away, and the average aggregates price is about USD 30.00 per ton at the quarry. There will be additional costs to get the aggregates transported to the point of use.

**Mr. Li:** Is there enough labor force in the area?

**Mr. Jonathan:** Plenty of. We have an abundant labor force across the whole country, but most of them only have preliminary-level education.

**Mr. Li:** Don't worry. We will set up training programs to teach them construction skills.

**Mr. Harold:** Wonderful! We need the skilled workers urgently for our nationwide reconstruction.

**Mr. Zhong:** What is the salary level of local workers?

**Mr. Jonathan:** The unskilled laborer is paid about USD 150.00 per month; the skilled worker is paid about USD 300.00 per month, while engineers are at a premium and their average salary is over USD 1,000.00 per month.

### Keywords & Expressions

| | |
|---|---|
| Pre-contract activities | 签约前期工作 |
| Site investigation | 现场踏勘 |
| Surveyor | 测量员，测量师 |
| Estimator | 估算师 |

| | |
|---|---|
| Accommodation | 食宿 |
| Veteran | 老手，老兵 |
| Count on | 依靠，指望 |
| Check list | 核对表，清单 |
| Topographic map | 地形图，等高线图 |
| Highway network master plan | 公路网总体规划图 |
| RTK (real-time kinematic) | 实时动态测量 |
| GPS (global position system) | 全球定位系统 |
| Design speed | 设计速度 |
| Curvature | 曲率 |
| Low-lying area | 低洼地 |
| Wetland | 湿地 |
| Terrain | 地形，地势 |
| Landform | 地形 |
| Precipitation record | 降水记录 |
| Rainstorm intensity formula | 暴雨强度公式 |
| Meteorological department | 气象局 |
| Be pooled | 汇集 |
| Detour | 绕道 |
| Steep gradients slope | 陡坡 |
| Sharp curvature | 急转弯 |
| Seasonal river | 季节性河流 |
| Diesel generator | 柴油发电机 |
| Quarry | 采石场 |
| Skilled worker | 熟练工人 |
| Unskilled laborer | 非熟练工人，力工 |
| Nationwide reconstruction | 全国范围的重建 |

# 第二章　BOT 项目签约前期工作

## 第 6 课　项目信息搜集与现场踏勘

### 对话 1

**李先生 - M 集团国际承包公司工程部经理**

**Harold 先生 - 基础设施建设部道路司司长**

**李先生：** 早上好，Harold 先生！很高兴再次见到您。

**Harold 先生：** 李先生早上好！我正等你安排现场踏勘的相关事宜呢。

**李先生：** 您每次都是雪中送炭啊。谢谢您，Harold 先生。昨天部长和我们的总裁就东西高速公路项目签署了谅解备忘录。进度计划安排得那么紧，我们必须马上开始工作啦。

**Harold 先生：** 是的，李先生。不过不用担心，昨天我就得到部长的指示，我就是来这里帮助你们的。我已经通知沿途各市的市政府，他们也将陪同我们，并尽一切努力为你们的踏勘提供便利。我将和你们团队沿这条路线一路同行。在开始现场踏勘之前，我们得好好准备。你们小组有多少人跟我同行啊？

**李先生**：我们有四个人。我是组长，组里还有一名设计师、一名测量员和一名估算师。

**Harold 先生**：我会通知沿途的官员为你们准备好食宿，但交通需要你们自己安排咯。

**李先生**：没问题。我会安排一辆吉普给我们一路使用。如果您能为我推荐一名熟悉地形对这段路线轻车熟道、有经验的老司机将对我们有很大帮助。这样的人可以帮助我们避免路途中的困难。

**Harold 先生**：当然，你就包在我身上吧。我的一位朋友向来是在公路网检查时为我们部开车的。会后我会给他打电话，今天下午他就会来找你们讨论相关安排及你们所需要的。

**李先生**：那太好了。那我们什么时候出发？明天出发行吗？

**Harold 先生**：明天不行。明天我有一个重要的会议。我想我们可以后天出发。预计我们将查看整个 450 公里的路线，所以我们必须做好充分准备。

**李先生**：您说的完全正确。我们已经就现场踏勘的准备事项列出一个清单。您看，其中两件东西，即地形图和公路网总体规划图，要您带来。

**Harold 先生**：我已经准备好了。我会记得把它们带来的。

**李先生**：我们会将 RTK、GPS 设备、野外勘测用的伞和必要的药品提前装上吉普车。您看我们还需要带别的什么吗？

**Harold 先生**：你想的真周到。

**李先生**：后天上午八点我会到贵部办公楼去接您的。

**Harold 先生**：就这么定了，到时候见。可记得带上你们的护照哦。

## 对话 2

**李先生** - M 集团国际承包公司工程部经理

**宋先生** - M 集团国际承包公司道路设计师

**钟先生** - M 集团国际承包公司估算师

**Harold 先生** - 基础设施建设部道路司司长

**Jonathan 先生** - 当地省长

**Jonathan 先生**：我们一直在察看这条路线的东段。你们都有什么问题吗？

**宋先生**：我确实有一个问题。根据原先的公路网规划和图纸，该公路的设计时速是每小时 120 公里。然而，设计的路线与速度并不匹配。很多地方的坡度太陡、转弯太急。那就意味着计划中的路线不是最优的，毫无疑问那将需要大量的土方工程。另外，我观察到一路上有低洼地和湿地，因此路基可能需要进行特殊处理。我建议派遣专门的地质勘探队伍对这些区域做进一步的调查。

**Harold 先生**：旧的总体规划是几十年之前一家欧洲公司编制的，与那时相比，现在的地形已经发生了很大变化，所以它也许已经不能反映当前的情况了。

**Jonathan 先生**：Harold 说得对。这里雨季的雨势非常大,导致了地形的变化。近年来,大雨造成的洪水淹没庄稼,甚至冲毁道路和桥梁。

**宋先生**：Harold 先生,请问我们在哪里可以得到这个地区的降水记录和暴雨强度公式呢?

**Harold 先生**：在首都的气象局保存着所有这些数据。等我们回到首都之后可以从他们那里购买这些资料。

**Jonathan 先生**：不好意思,我希望这条新的高速公路规划通过 T 市,那是我们省的一个新发展起来的城市。该地区越来越多的大量高价值的农产品都集中到那里,需要出口到国外去。

**宋先生**：让我看看地图。啊,在这里。绕行 T 市正好可以规避该地区的陡坡和急转弯的问题。

**Jonathan 先生**：哦,那可真是个好消息!

**李先生**：我有一个关于水源的问题。筑路需要消耗大量的水。附近有合适的水源吗?

**Jonathan 先生**：R 河离这个路段大约 20 公里。

**李先生**：R 河的水量和水质怎么样?是不是一条季节性河流?

**Jonathan 先生**：哦,不用担心。R 河是我国的主要河流之一,它一年四季都保持着巨大的流量。它的水量应该可以满足建设的需要。

**李先生**：好!我们将对此作进一步的勘查。施工用电的供应怎么样啊?

**Jonathan 先生**：我省多年以来一直面临严重的电力短缺。对你们的电力需求我无能为力。你们只能用柴油发电机为施工供电。

国家石油公司能将柴油送至当地现场。

**李先生：** 当地可有沥青和骨料啊？如有的话，你知道价格是多少吗？

**Harold 先生：** 我们国家还没有沥青厂。沥青都需要从国外进口。在 100 公里外的山区有许多采石场，在采石场骨料的平均价格是每吨 30 美元。将骨料运送到使用地点还需要额外的费用。

**李先生：** 这个地区有足够的劳动力吗？

**Jonathan 先生：** 很多很多。整个国家到处都有充沛的劳动力资源，不过大多数人只受到过初等教育。

**李先生：** 那不用担心，我们会开设培训计划，教他们施工技能。

**Harold 先生：** 好极了！我们急需熟练工人来进行全国范围的重建。

**钟先生：** 当地工人的工资水平是多少？

**Jonathan 先生：** 非熟练工人大约每月 150 美元，熟练工人大约每月 300 美元，而工程师工资较高，他们的月薪则超过 1000 美元。

## LESSON 7  CONCEPTUAL DESIGN

**Dialogue 1**

**Mr. Song-Road Designer of International Contracting Company of Group M**

**Mr. Harold-Director of Road Department of the Ministry of Infrastructure Development**

**Mr. Song:** Good morning, Mr. Harold. Thank you for your support guiding us along the proposed highway route, it really helped us with our survey. We have completed the first version of the conceptual design according to the master plan and the site inspection, I hope to discuss that with you today.

**Mr. Harold:** Sure, you're so efficient. Let's get started.

**Mr. Song:** According to your old 1 : 10000 topographic map, master plan, relevant technical documents, our recent site investigation, the current traffic conditions and the projections for future economic development in the region, we believe that a two-way, four-lane highway is required now. And a space for further two lanes would be reserved for capacity expansion.

**Mr. Harold:** Have you made traffic volume analysis to support the highway configuration you are recommending?

**Mr. Song:** Of course we have. We've surveyed the current passenger traffic and freight traffic volume, and converted all the different types of vehicles into passenger car units. Then we undertook a traffic volume analysis in PCU/h and informed by that study we decides the optimum highway lane configuration.

**Mr. Harold:** That's good. I agree with your proposal in respect of the lanes arrangement. But I notice some changes have been made to the original plan. May I hear the reasons behind?

**Mr. Song:** Well, I did make some adjustments to the original plan. Some sections like K220–K270 crossed the areas with complicated terrain, so I rerouted these sections to relatively flat ground so as to avoid unnecessary earthwork.

**Mr. Harold:** What about the sections of K100–K130 and K150–K180?

**Mr. Song:** I altered K100–K130 to minimize the land acquisition from the adjacent farms. K150–K180 of the original route was within area considered to be bad from a geological perspective. The new route shown of the drawing bypasses these areas, it reduces the number of bridges. With this proposed route we anticipate fewer construction difficulties, which will reduce the cost and time for construction.

**Mr. Harold:** That's great. Have you considered the governor's suggestion of passing by City T?

**Mr. Song:** Of course. More than that, we have paid many attention to how the highway can serve all the main towns along the route as well as put consideration on the cross relations of your country's whole road network.

**Mr. Harold:** That's a very professional approach. Since there are many changes, I wonder whether the total length and cost are increased or not.

**Mr. Song:** The overall effect is not detrimental. Although the total length of the highway has increased, we have optimized the design, so the overall cost should not be increased much.

**Mr. Harold:** That's fantastic. I don't have any other questions on the proposed route. This afternoon we will discuss the road structure, is that correct?

**Mr. Song:** Yes. Let's resume our discussions after lunch.

## Dialogue 2

**Mr. Song-Road Designer of International Contracting Company of Group M**

**Mr. Harold-Director of Road Department of the Ministry of Infrastructure Development**

**Mr. Harold:** Good afternoon, Mr. Song! Can we start by taking a look at some cross sectional drawings?

**Mr. Song:** Yes, of course, here you are. Firstly, I would like to describe the road structure. The subgrade will comprise sand gravels 20 cm thick. The sub-base is cement stabilized gravels 18 cm thick, and the base course is cement stabilized gravels 20 cm thick. The road surface will be asphalt concrete 5+7+5 cm thick.

**Mr. Harold:** The proposed structure is a good design, but I have a small suggestion for you. My suggestion is to change the base course to graded crushed stone. From our experience, if you use cement stabilized gravels, the road will crack easily due to wide temperature differences and the effect of intense direct sunshine. Graded crushed stone is a much better solution for the local situation and can prevent the road from cracking.

**Mr. Song:** Thanks for your advice, Mr. Harold. Your knowledge and suggestion is very valuable to us. I will modify the specifications accordingly. We have noticed that there are many aggregate resources along the route. We plan to make further tests on their quality to find out whether they can meet the requirements of our highway.

**Mr. Harold:** That's good. Another question has just occurred to me. How do you plan to deal with the side slopes?

**Mr. Song:** Where the gradient is less than 25 degrees, we plan to stabilize the slope using slope green method; if the gradient is between 25 and 40 degrees, we plan to use stone masonry to provide stability. If the gradient is over 40 degrees, we will install anchor bolts support and then stabilize the slope with shotcrete.

**Mr. Harold:** Good. I have just noticed that on the drawing of the right corner it includes a specification reference JTG B01-2014. What is that specification?

**Mr. Song**: Oh, this is the Chinese technical standard for highway engineering. The whole design is based on this standard.

**Mr. Harold**: That's interesting. In your standard, what is the required Coefficient of Compacting and CBR?

**Mr. Song**: The coefficient of compaction for this kind of highway is 0.96 and CBR is 8.

**Mr. Harold**: I suggest it is better to adopt the EU Standard which our country normally uses. In the EU Standard I recall that the coefficient of compaction is 0.98 and CBR is 10 in EU Standard.

**Mr. Song**: I understand your concern, but it may not be necessary to use EU Standard. The Chinese Standard was initially based on other international standards, including the British Standard, the EU Standard, and the US Standard. Our experience has allowed us to keep the strengths of international standards, and optimize them. The Chinese standard has not only regulated the whole construction engineering circle in China, but also adopted and proved very successful in many other countries, such as X and Y in your continent. So, I believe the Chinese Standard is no problem.

**Mr. Harold**: I accept that the Chinese Standard is being used more and more internationally. But our engineers and supervisors are not familiar with the Chinese Standard at present. It will cause difficulties in our communication. Our supervisor is from Country Z of this continent, I suggest we'd better adopt their standard.

**Mr. Song**: I know the idiom "When in Rome, do as the Romans do". Therefore, we will follow your advice, which we appreciate.

We have undertaken a road project in Country Z as well. So we are quite familiar with Country Z's standard for highway design and construction.

**Mr. Harold:** Oh, good! We've found a solution that meets both our needs.

**Mr. Song:** We will revise our conceptual design according to Country Z's standard and submit it again for your review and approval.

## Keywords & Expressions

| | |
|---|---|
| Conceptual design | 概念设计 |
| Topographic map | 地形图 |
| Two-way, four-lane highway | 双向四车道的公路 |
| Traffic volume analysis | 交通量分析 |
| Lanes arrangement | 车道布置 |
| Passenger traffic volume | 客运交通量 |
| Freight traffic volume | 货运交通量 |
| PCU (passenger car unit) | 标准车当量数（以客运小轿车为单位） |
| PCU/h | 每小时通过的标准车当量数 |
| Complicated terrain | 复杂地形 |
| Land acquisition | 土地征用 |
| Cross relations | 交叉关系 |
| Road structure | 道路结构 |
| Subgrade | 路基 |
| Sub-base | 底基层 |
| Base course | 层 |
| Sand gravel | 沙砾 |
| Cement stabilized gravels | 水泥稳定砾石 |
| Asphalt concrete | 沥青混凝土 |

| | |
|---|---|
| Graded crushed stone | 级配碎石 |
| Slope green method | 绿植护坡法 |
| Stone masonry | 砌石 |
| Anchor bolt support | 锚杆支护 |
| Shotcrete | 喷射混凝土 |
| Coefficient of compact | 压实系数 |
| CBR (California Bearing Ratio) | 加州承载比 |
| EU Standard | 欧洲标准 |
| British Standard | 英国标准 |
| US Standard | 美国标准 |
| When in Rome, do as the Romans do | 入乡随俗 |

# 第 7 课　概念设计

## 对话 1

宋先生 - M 集团国际承包公司道路设计师
Harold 先生 - 基础设施建设部道路司司长

**宋先生：** Harold 先生早上好！谢谢您上次一路引领我们考察建议的路线，对我们的测量工作帮助很大。我们已经依据总体规划和实地踏勘完成了概念设计的初稿，我希望今天就此与您讨论。

**Harold 先生：** 好啊！你们效率这么高啊！那我们就开始吧。

**宋先生：** 根据你们原先的万分之一地形图、总体规划、相关的技术资料、我们近期的现场调查、当前的交通情况以及对本地区未来经济发展的预测，我认为建一条双向四车道的公路是很合适的，另外为今后扩建再留出两个车道的空间。

**Harold 先生**：你做了交通量分析来支持你所建议的高速公路配置了吗？

**宋先生**：我们当然做了。我们调查了当前的客运量和货运量，并将所有不同类型的车辆都折算成小客车为单位。然后，我们以标准车当量数进行了流量分析并据此确定了高速公路的最优车道布置。

**Harold 先生**：很好。那我就同意你的车道安排。不过我注意到原来的平面图有了一些变化啊。我可以听听背后的原因吗？

**宋先生**：嗯，我确实对原来的平面图做了一些调整。一些路段，比如 K220-K270，跨越了地形复杂的地区，所以我把这些路段改到相对平坦的地面，以避免不必要的土方工程。

**Harold 先生**：那么 K100-K130 和 K150-K180 路段呢？

**Song 先生**：我改动 K100-K130 路段以尽量减少从周边农场征地。原来 K150-K180 的线路处在地质条件恶劣的地区。图纸上的新路线则绕过了这些区域，减少了桥梁的数量。这条建议的路线预计将减小施工难度，并减少施工成本和施工时间。

**Harold 先生**：那太好了！你考虑过州长关于经过 T 市的建议了吗？

**Song 先生**：当然！不仅如此，我们在高速公路如何服务沿线的各主要城镇方面倾注了很多关注，还考虑到与贵国整个公路网的交叉关系。

**Harold 先生**：你做事的方式很专业啊。既然有那么多变化，我想知道总长度和费用是否都增加了。

**宋先生**：那倒不见得。高速公路的总长度显然是增加了，不过我们做了设计优化，所以总成本应该不会增加太多。

**Harold 先生**：太棒了！对于建议线路我们没有任何问题了。今天下午我们要讨论道路结构了，是这样吧？

**宋先生**：是的。我们午饭后继续讨论吧。

## 对话 2

**宋先生 - M 集团国际承包公司道路设计师**

**Harold 先生 - 基础设施建设部道路司司长**

**Harold 先生**：宋先生下午好！我们可以先看一下道路断面图吗？

**宋先生**：当然可以，给您断面图。首先我想向您解释一下道路结构。路基是 20 厘米厚的砂砾。底基层是 18 厘米厚的水泥稳定砾石，而基层是 20 厘米厚的水泥稳定砾石。道路面层是 5+7+5 厘米厚的沥青混凝土。

**Harold 先生**：这个建议道路结构设计的挺好，不过我有一个小建议要给你，那就是把基层改为级配碎石。根据我们的经验，如果你们用水泥稳定砾石，由于昼夜温差显著、日照强烈，道路容易开裂；而级配碎石更适于当地的情况，能够防止路面开裂。

**宋先生**：谢谢您的指点，Harold 先生。您的学识和建议对我们非常有价值。我会作相应的修改。我们已经注意到沿线有很多石料资源。我们计划对它们的质量作进一步试验来确定它们能否满足我们高速路的要求。

Harold 先生：那就好。我刚想起另外一个问题，你们打算如何处理边坡？

宋先生：坡度在 25° 以内之处，我们计划采用绿植护坡法；如果坡度在 25°~40° 之间，我们计划用砌石提供稳定性；如果坡度大于 40°，我们将安装锚杆支护之后使用喷射混凝土稳定边坡。

Harold 先生：好。我刚刚注意到图的右下角提及采用的规范是 JTG B01-2014。那是什么规范啊？

宋先生：噢，这是中国公路工程的技术标准。整个设计就是基于这个标准。

Harold 先生：这很有趣，在你们的标准里对压实系数和加州承载比的要求是多少？

宋先生：压实系数是 0.96，加州承载比是 8。

Harold 先生：我建议还是采用我们国家常规采用的欧洲规范为好。据我记得欧洲规范里的压实系数为 0.98 而加州承载比是 10。

宋先生：我理解您的关注，不过我并不认为有必要采用欧洲规范。中国标准最初是基于其他国际标准的，包括英国标准、欧洲标准和美国标准。我们的经验使我们汲取了它们的长处并加以优化。中国标准不仅规范着整个中国建筑工程界，而且在很多别的国家也被证明相当成功，比如在你们这个洲的 X 国和 Y 国。因此，我认为中国标准是没有问题的。

Harold 先生：我承认中国标准已经在全世界越来越广泛地得以应用。但是目前我们的工程师和监理人员对中国标准都还不熟悉。这将导致我们的沟通困难。我们的监理人员来自本洲的 Z 国，我建议我们最好采用他们的标准。

**宋先生**：我知道入乡随俗这个成语，所以您的建议我欣然接受。我们在 Z 国也曾有过一个道路工程，所以我们对该国的标准相当熟悉。

**Harold 先生**：噢，那好啊！我们找到了满足我们双方需求的完美方案。

**宋先生**：我们会按照 Z 国标准修改我们的概念设计并提交给您审阅、批准。

# LESSON 8  FEASIBILITY STUDY & ENVIRONMENTAL IMPACT ASSESSMENT

**Dialogue 1**

**Mr. Bai-President of International Contracting Company of Group M**

**Mr. Li-Director of Engineering Department of International Contracting Company of Group M**

**Mr. Fernando-Minister, Ministry of Infrastructure Development**

**Mr. Fernando:** Mr. Bai, today I would like you to present your report on the proposed highway feasibility study, which is very important to us. An important principle is that West-east Highway Project will generate sufficient cash flow to cover all the costs of construction and operation. We agreed that the feasibility study shall evaluate all aspects of the project to determine if the highway project is feasible economically, environmentally and socially.

**Mr. Bai:** We understand that the feasibility study is really important. In fact, its conclusions will determine if we can proceed with the required investment. Accordingly, we have undertaken series of in-depth investigations, collected a large amount of data, and organized many experts in different areas to ensure the accuracy and creditability of the highway feasibility study. Mr. Li, the director of our companies' Engineering Department will initially summarize the feasibility study for you.

**Mr. Li:** Honorable minister, our Feasibility Study Report is composed of fourteen sections covering General Description of the Project, Necessity of the Project, Present Economy/Society/Transportation Conditions and Development Plan, Traffic Volume Analysis and Prediction, Technical Specification and Construction Proposal of the Project, Operation & Maintenance Proposal, Investment Estimation and Financing, Economic and Financial Evaluation, Environmental & Social Impact Assessment, Risk Analysis and Conclusion.

**Mr. Fernando:** The Ministry of Transportation knows well of the current situation and understand the transportation development plan. I suggest that initially you focus on discussing the economic and financial evaluation.

**Mr. Li:** Okay. Investigation shows that the average traffic flow rate of Road R1 is 6,000 pcu/d. According to historical record, the traffic flow rate has increased by 6% annually in each of the last five years. The existing two-lane road is in bad condition and can no longer meet the actual needs. When the West-east highway is completed in five years, the average traffic flow rate will be about 7,575 pcu/d. In five years, the traffic growth rate is expected to slow down gradually. Whereas the economy of Country A is full of potential, in line with the calculation under our prediction model, the traffic flow rate will still reach about 10,000 and 15,000 pcu/d 10 years and 20 years later respectively.

**Mr. Fernando:** Tell me how you analyze the financial feasibility of the project please.

**Mr. Li:** Okay. The financial feasibility was analyzed on the base of foregoing chapters, especially upon the data related to traffic volume prediction, the construction cost/operation expense estimation, the financial cost calculation and the income predictionm, etc. We consolidated all the above financial data into the Chart of Funds Flow covering 5 years' construction period and 25 years' operation period. The expenditure of the project was analyzed under two categories of Capex and Opex respectively.

**Mr. Fernando:** What is IRR according to your analysis?

**Mr. Li:** Based on the 25-year operation period economic cost-benefit analysis, we predict that the internal rate of return of the project is 15%. According to our economic cost-benefit sensitivity analysis, in the adverse case of 10% traffic flow reduction and a 10% increase in commodity prices, the internal rate of return will drop to 8%. From the economic cost-benefit perspective, the Project is just basically feasible.

**Mr. Fernando:** What assumptions have you made in respect of toll fees?

**Mr. Li:** According to our financial analysis, we plan to divide

## CHAPTER II  PRE-CONTRACT ACTIVITIES OF BOT PROJECT

the vehicles into three categories: large, medium and small. We currently plan to charge USD 0.30 per km for large vehicles, USD 0.20 per km for medium vehicles and USD 0.15 per km for small vehicles.

**Mr. Fernando:** I think your rates are high. At present we are an undeveloped country and our economy is still at a low level, high toll fees will be a drag on our economic development. I suggest USD 0.20 per km for large vehicles, USD 0.15 per km for medium vehicles and USD 0.10 per km for small vehicles.

**Mr. Bai:** I understand your concern, minister. But it will be hard for us to cover the financial and operating costs if the toll rates are reduced so much. It will become impossible to get investment finance from the financing institutions.

**Mr. Fernando:** Don't worry about that just at the minute. There are two ways we can alleviate any financial distress. The first is that before the traffic flow rate reaches the break-even point, the government promises to provide compensation for any losses. The second is that we can provide certain land at no cost along the route to allow you to undertake real estate development.

**Mr. Bai:** These suggestions remove a great burden. We are so relieved to hear your proposals. We will re-calculate the break-even point and reissue the Feasibility Study Report incorporating your proposals.

**Mr. Fernando:** How do you plan to raise the funds for the project?

**Mr. Li:** Our current thinking is that 20% of the total construction cost will be funded by our company. For the remainder we are planned to seek finance from the International Infrastructure Investment Corporation, Asian Infrastructure Investment Bank, the Belt and

Road Fund and relevant Chinese financial institutions etc. At the same time, we would like you to consider if your government wants to invest in the highway development investing money, and setting up a joint project company with us working together.

**Mr. Fernando:** Our country is still in a very difficult economic position. There is tremendous pressure to minimize current expenditure; the government has a very tight budget. We will not be able to participate as an investment partner. However, since the project is critical to our country's development, the government will certainly give full support by providing some preferential policies and tax exemptions to assist the implementation and operation of the project.

**Mr. Bai:** That's wonderful. The things you have mentioned have made me more confident than ever about this project being successful.

**Mr. Fernando:** If we want a successful project, the environment must be taken into account as far as possible. So another important part of the project is the environmental impact assessment. I would like to invite an official from the Ministry of Environment Protection to give his professional advice and opinion. Are you available tomorrow for this special meeting?

**Mr. Bai:** No problem, Minister. See you tomorrow.

## Dialogue 2

## Mr. Bai-President of International Contracting Company of Group M

CHAPTER II  PRE-CONTRACT ACTIVITIES OF BOT PROJECT

**Mr. Fernando-Minister, Ministry of Infrastructure Development**
**Mr. Martin-Official, Ministry of Environment Protection**
**Mr. Francis-Expert, Local Environmental Assessment Company**

**Mr. Bai:** Before we present our environmental impact assessment, I would like to introduce Mr. Francis, an expert from a local environmental assessment company. He has helped us to compile the environmental impact assessment.

**Mr. Francis:** Good morning, honorable minister, Mr. Martin. Please allow me to report on the environmental impact assessment. It is inevitable that the construction of a highway will have an environmental impact. What is important is to ensure that any environmental impact is anticipated, controlled, managed and mitigated. Environmental factors which can have a possible impact on the ecology and environment along the highway route, include atmosphere, ecology, noise, water, social environment and so on. In general, our assessment of the measures proposed by Mr. Bai's company, demonstrates a commitment to control the overall impact on the environment to an acceptable level. Mr. Bai's company has proposed effective and practicable measures to minimize the environmental impacts both from a design perspective and construction perspective. For example, considering design, the original route planned for the highway would pass land adjacent to wetlands under ecological environment protection; they changed the route of the highway so that it would bypass the ecological zone by some considerable distance. Considering construction, Mr. Bai's company will adopt sprinkler during road construction to reduce dust. Moreover, all trees with a DBH over 10 cm that will be adversely affected by the construction will be transplanted, chopping down is prohibited. Therefore damage to the ecology and vegetation will be reduced as far as possible.

**Mr. Martin:** Okay. I noticed that concrete batching plants will be set during construction. How will you deal with their waste water?

**Mr. Francis:** A sedimentation basin will be built as an integral part of each batching plant to collect the waste water, and the batching plant water shall be discharged only after the sedimentation process.

**Mr. Martin:** Good. Since this is a BOT project, what measures do you plan to take for protecting the environment during the operation stage?

**Mr. Francis:** To prevent the noise pollution, trees will be planted along the route for noise absorption. Sewage treatment facilities will be arranged at toll gates and service stations to ensure the waste water being properly treated before being discharged.

**Mr. Martin:** Very well! This highway runs from West to East across the whole country, which cuts off the passage of the horizontal migration of wild animals. How will you solve this problem?

**Mr. Francis:** Good question! We have collected data of the wild animal activities on both sides of the highway using belt transect monitoring and field research which has given us clearer picture of the abundance and presence of different species. To minimize the impact to wild animals, bridges or culverts are planned for the safe migration and diffusion of wild animals.

**Mr. Martin:** Excellent! You are the true professionals. I suppose that they have taken everything into consideration. I don't have any other questions, Minister.

**Mr. Fernando:** If the Ministry of Environment Protection is satisfied, I don't have any objection. Mr. Bai, please formally submit your final feasibility study and environmental assessment report to the Ministry of Infrastructure Development before the end of this week. We will submit the two documents to the Cabinet for discussion and approval. Mr. Martin, I hope the Ministry of Environment Protection will press the "Yes" button in the cabinet meeting.

**Mr. Bai & Mr. Martin:** Yes, Minister!

## Key Words & Expressions

| | |
|---|---|
| Feasibility Study | 可行性研究 |
| Accuracy | 准确度 |
| Creditability | 可信度 |
| Environmental & Social Impact Assessment | 环境和社会影响评估 |
| Economic and Financial Evaluation | 经济和财务评价 |
| Traffic flow rate | 交通流率 |
| Pcu/d | 每天通过的标准车数量 |
| In line with | 根据 |
| Prediction model | 预测模型 |
| Chart of Funds Flow | 资金流量图表 |
| Capex (capital expenditures) | 资本支出 |
| Opex (operational expenditures) | 运营支出 |
| IRR (Internal Rate of Return) | 内部收益率 |
| Economic cost-benefit analysis | 经济成本效益分析 |
| In the adverse case | 在不利情况下 |
| Toll fee | 通行费，高速费 |
| Break-even point | 盈亏平衡点 |
| International Infrastructure Investment | |

| | |
|---|---|
| Corporation | 国际基础设施投资公司 |
| Asian Infrastructure Investment Bank | 亚洲基础设施投资银行 |
| Belt and Road Fund | 一带一路基金 |
| Financial institution | 金融机构 |
| Preferential policy | 优惠政策 |
| Tax exemptions | 免税 |
| Ecology (ecological) | 生态,(生态的) |
| Atmosphere | 大气 |
| Transplant | 移植 |
| DBH (diameter at breast height) | 胸径 |
| Chop down | 砍伐 |
| Concrete batching plant | 混凝土搅拌站 |
| Sedimentation basin | 沉淀池 |
| Noise pollution | 噪声污染 |
| Noise absorption | 吸收噪声 |
| Sewage treatment facilities | 污水处理设施 |
| Toll gate | 收费站,收费口 |
| Horizontal migration | 水平迁徙 |
| Belt transect monitoring | 样带检测 |
| Diffusion | 扩散 |
| Cabinet | 内阁 |

# 第 8 课　可行性研究和环境影响评价

## 对话 1

**白先生 - M 集团国际承包公司总裁**

**李先生 - M 集团国际承包公司工程部经理**

**Fernando 先生 - 基础设施建设部部长**

**Fernando 先生：**白先生，今天我想听听你们对拟建高速公路的可行性研究报告，这对我们非常重要。一个最重要的原则是东西高速公路项目要产生足够的现金流，以覆盖其施工和运营全部成本。我们达成共识，可行性研究应从所有角度来评价项目，以确定这个项目在经济、环境和社会方面是否都可行。

**白先生：**我们理解可行性研究的重要性。事实上，它的结论将决定我们能否获得所需的投资。因此，我们做了一系列的深度调查，收集了大量数据，并组织了各个领域的专家来保证这个可行性研究的准确性和可信度。我们公司工程部总经理李先生将首先向您概述一下该可行性研究。

**李先生：**尊敬的部长，我们的可行性研究报告由 14 个部分组成，包括：项目概述、项目的必要性、经济/社会/交通现状与发展规划、交通量分析与预测、技术规格与项目建设方案、运营维护方案、投资估算与融资、经济与财务评价、环境与社会影响评估、风险分析以及结论。

**Fernando 先生：**交通部对当前状况和交通发展规划很清楚。我建议你的汇报聚焦到经济和财务评价。

**李先生：**好的。调查显示 R1 公路的平均交通流率为每天 6000 辆标准车。根据历史记录，在过去的五年里交通流率每年增长 6%；而现存的两车道路况很差，再也满足不了现实的需求。五年之后当东西高速公路完工的时候，平均交通流率约将为每天 7575 辆标准车。此后，交通流量的增速有望逐渐放缓。鉴于 A 国经济充满潜能，按我们的预测模型计算，10 年和 20 年之后交通流率仍将分别达到每天 1 万和 1.5 万辆标准车。

**Fernando 先生：**请让我知道你是怎么做项目的财务可行性分析的吧。

**李先生：**行。财务可行性是基于前述各章来进行分析的，特别是依据交通流量预测、建设成本与运营费用测算、财务成本计算以及收入预测等数据。我们将上述所有财务数据都汇总为一张覆盖 5 年建设期和 25 年运营期的资金流量图表。项目开支分为资本支出和运营支出两大类分别进行分析。

**Fernando 先生：**根据你的分析，内部收益率是多少？

**李先生：**基于 25 年运营期经济成本效益分析，我们预估项目的内部收益率为 15%。根据经济成本效益敏感性分析，在车流量下降10%并且日用品价格有10%上升的不利情况下，内部收益率将下降至8%。从经济成本效益的角度，这刚刚算是个基本可行的项目。

**Fernando 先生**：过路费你们是怎么假设的？

**李先生**：根据我们的财务分析，我们计划把车辆划分为大型车、中型车和小型车三大类。目前我们打算对大型车辆征收每千米0.30美元，重型车辆每千米0.20美元，小型车辆每千米0.15美元。

**Fernando 先生**：我认为你们的收费高了。当前我们国家还是个发展中国家，经济还处于一个低水平，高过路费会拖累我们的经济。我建议大型车辆每千米收0.20美元，中型车辆0.15美元，小型车辆0.10美元。

**白先生**：部长，我理解您的担心。但是如果过路费减少得太多，对我们来说财务费用和运营成本就难以覆盖，这样从融资机构获得投融资是不可能的。

**Fernando 先生**：现在我们先不担心这个。我们有两种方法可以缓解任何财务困境。第一是在交通流率达到盈亏平衡点之前，政府承诺来补偿损失；第二是我们可以在沿线为你们的房地产开发免费提供一些地块。

**白先生**：这些建议消除了很大的担忧。听到您的建议我们松了一口气。我们会结合您的建议，重新测算盈亏平衡点并重新发布可行性研究报告。

**Fernando 先生**：你们打算如何筹措资金呢？

**李先生**：我们目前的想法是建设费用的20%将由我们公司投资。其余部分打算从国际基础设施投资公司、亚洲基础设施投资银行、一带一路基金以及相关的中国金融机构寻求融资。同时，我们希望您考虑政府可以放入部分投资，和我们合作共同设立项目公司。

**Fernando 先生**：我们国家仍处于经济困难之中。最大限度地减少经常性开支的压力巨大；政府预算捉襟见肘。我们对参与项目投资无能为力啊。但是，既然这个项目对我国至关重要，政府当然要通过提供某些优惠政策和免税对项目的实施和运营给予全力的支持。

**白先生**：这非常好。听了您这番话，我比以往任何时候对这个项目的成功更有信心了。

**Fernando 先生**：这个项目要想成功，就必须尽可能地考虑到环境因素。所以项目的另一个重要的部分是项目的环境影响评价，我想邀请环境保护部的官员给一些专业的意见。你明天能再来参加这一专题会议吗？

**白先生**：没问题，部长。明天见。

## 对话 2

**白先生 -M 集团国际承包公司总裁**

**Fernando 先生 - 基础设施建设部部长**

**Martin 先生 - 环境保护部官员**

**Francis 先生 - 当地环境评价公司专家**

**白先生**：在陈述我们的环境影响评价之前，我想介绍一位本地环境评价公司的专家 Francis 先生，他帮助我们编制了环境影响评价。

**Francis 先生**：尊敬的部长，Martin 先生，早上好。请允许我来汇报环境影响评价。高速公路项目建设不可避免地会对环境产生影响。重要的是确保任何环境影响都是可预测、可控制、可管理和可减轻的。影响公路沿线生态环境的环境因素包括大气、生态、噪声、水、社会环境等。总的来说，我们对白先生公司所采取的措施作的评估表明，他们致力对环境的总体影响控制在可接受的水平。白先生的公司从设计和施工的角度提出了切实有效的措施，将对环境的影响降至最低。例如从设计上考虑，原设计路线要经过一些生态环境保护的湿地，他们改变了路线绕过了生态区并保持合适的距离。考虑到施工，在道路施工期间中国人将洒水降尘；此外，所有受施工影响的胸径 10 厘米以上的树木一律移栽、不准砍伐。那样对生态和植被的损毁将得以尽可能地降低。

**Martin 先生**：不错。我注意到施工期间将设立若干混凝土搅拌站。你们将如何处置搅拌站废水呢？

**Francis 先生**：作为整体的一部分，每座搅拌站都会建设一个沉淀池来收集废水，搅拌站的水只有经过沉淀处理之后才会排放。

**Martin 先生**：好的。既然这是一个 BOT 项目，在运营阶段你们打算采取什么样的措施来保护环境？

**Francis 先生**：为了防止噪声污染，沿线将种植树木以吸收噪声。在收费口和服务站将设置污水处理设施，保证污水在排放之前得以恰当处理。

**Martin 先生**：非常好！这条高速公路东西横跨整个国家，切断了野生动物南北迁徙的通道。你们如何解决这一问题呢？

**Francis 先生**：问得好！我们通过样带检测和湿地调研采集了高速路两侧野生动物的活动数据，使我们更清楚地了解到不同物种的丰富度和呈现状态。为了将对野生动物的影响减至最低，规划了桥梁和涵洞让野生动物安全地迁徙和扩散。

**Martin 先生：** 好极了！你是一位真正的专家。我认为他们已经把所有问题都考虑到了。部长，我没有其他问题了。

**Fernando 先生：** 如果环境保护部满意了，我没有异议。白先生，请在本周内将可行性研究报告和环境影响评估的最终版本提交到基础设施建设部。我们会将这两份文件提交到内阁讨论、批准。Martin 先生，我希望环境保护部在内阁会议上按下"赞成"键。

**白先生和 Martin 先生：** 好的，部长！

# LESSON 9  SEEKING FINANCE FOR THE PROJECT

## Dialogue

**Mr. Han**-CFO of International Contracting Company of Group M
**Mr. Zheng**-General Manager of Global Finance Department of A Famous Chinese Commercial Bank
**Mr. Hardaway**-State Secretary of Treasury Ministry of Country A

**Mr. Han:**  Good morning, Mr. Zheng.

**Mr. Zheng:**  Good morning, Mr. Han. What brings you here? And why are you talking with me in English instead of Mandarin?

**Mr. Han:**  I come here today with a friend of mine from country A. This is Mr. Hardaway, the State Secretary of Treasury Ministry of Country A.

**Mr. Zheng:** Nice to meet you, Mr. Hardaway. Welcome to our bank. Aha, Mr. Han, I guess you must have a new project under consideration.

**Mr. Han:** You know me best, Mr. Zheng. Yes, our company is going to develop the West-east Highway in Country A. The feasibility study has been approved by the Cabinet of the country. Mr. Hardaway and me are here to explore if your bank might become involved providing finance for the project.

**Mr. Zheng:** Oh, I know Country A. Mr. Hardaway, your country is a rising star in Continent H, which our bank is paying close attention to.

**Mr. Hardaway:** I am glad to know that you have knowledge about my country. It is appreciated. I believe our country can be considered like an eagle ready to take off, an eagle which is just looking for updraft, i.e. the finance.

**Mr. Zheng:** You've just made an appropriate and beautiful parable, Mr. Hardaway. I totally agree with you. May I know the contract amount and the implementation model of the project? Is it the F+EPC model you are considering?

**Mr. Han:** No, Mr. Zheng. This is a BOT project; the contract amount is approximately USD 4.8 billion.

**Mr. Zheng:** It is a mega project indeed. Do you think the government of the country will provide a sovereign guarantee for the project?

**Mr. Hardaway:** I am sorry, Mr. Zheng. Our government is not able to provide sovereign guarantee in relation to any loan for this project. We have to fulfill our commitments on the previous sovereign guarantees before issuing new ones.

**Mr. Han:** What Mr. Hardaway said is entirely true. Hence we are planning to establish a SPV locally and provide finance guarantee under its name.

**Mr. Zheng:** As it's a commercial project, I have to say that the guarantee from the SPV may not be enough; I think it is better for your company to provide a full-recourse guarantee for this project.

**Mr. Han:** According to our financial guidelines, our company is not able to provide a full-recourse guarantee anyway.

**Mr. Zheng:** What kind of collateral can be provided by the SPV then? You should understand, instead of being backed by a sovereign guarantee, you are entering a model of mortgage.

**Mr. Han:** Oh, I understand. We are going to take the anticipated income of the West-East Highway as the collateral. Our feasibility study shows the IRR will be above 12% and the project is able to generate real cash flow and a decent profit.

**Mr. Zheng:** It sounds acceptable, if the IRR prediction is reliable.

**Mr. Hardaway:** Our government has promised to compensate the SPV before the project reaches its break-even point.

**Mr. Zheng:** In this case, Mr. Han, my bank will consider making a compromise to accept a limited-recourse completion guarantee to cover the risk of cost over-run and construction delay risk. In the event the SPV is not able to complete the project on time, your company will be responsible to reimburse the debt on behalf of the SPV.

**Mr. Han:** It sounds more reasonable.

**Mr. Zheng:** By the way, can you confirm the finance structure for this project?

**Mr. Han**: The project is currently structured to have a conventional project finance arrangement with a debt equity ratio of 75/25. This means 25% of the total investment is from our company and the other 75% should be financed from the financial institution. We are seeking a 15-year long-term loan with a 5-year grace period for the project.

**Mr. Hardaway**: I wonder what interest rate you may provide for such project.

**Mr. Zheng**: At present our infrastructure interest rate is Libor+400.

**Mr. Han**: I care more about whether your bank might have the willingness to provide the whole loan we need or not?

**Mr. Zheng**: Our bank is interested in providing a loan for your West-east Highway Project. However, since this project is huge and the loan period is long, I think it can only be backed by a banking consortium.

**Mr. Hardaway**: Do you mean you are proposing a syndicated loan?

**Mr. Zheng**: You are right. My bank will take the role of lead lender and find other banks and financial institutions to provide the loan for this project together.

**Mr. Hardaway**: You are so helpful, Mr. Zheng!

**Mr. Han**: Mr. Zheng, would it be possible for you to send me a letter of confirming your interest to become involved with providing finance for the West-East highway project.

**Mr. Zheng**: Yes, I will send you a letter of interest this afternoon.

## CHAPTER II  PRE-CONTRACT ACTIVITIES OF BOT PROJECT

**Mr. Hardaway:** How long do you envisage from the issue of a statement of interest letter to the project financing close?

**Mr. Zheng:** Normally it will take 8 to 10 months.

**Mr. Hardaway:** This seems like a very long time. The Cabinet of my country is waiting for a commitment to offer a loan so that we can start the negotiation of the Concession Agreement.

**Mr. Zheng:** Our bank will issue a Letter of Intention to provide project finance soon after we reach an agreement on the critical terms of the financing agreement.

**Mr. Han:** Our wish is to move quickly to discuss the specific terms of the financing agreement.

**Mr. Zheng:** Okay, we can start our detailed discussions next week. May I mention something important? A prerequisite for overseas financing from our bank is overseas investment insurance. This should correspond with the risk rating of the relevant country and which covers political instability and unrest, exchange restrictions, risk of expropriation, unilateral termination of the contract or the concession agreement, war, etc.

**Mr. Hardaway:** Thanks for mentioning this. Can you introduce us to an insurance company that deal with such matters?

**Mr. Zheng:** SINOSURE, Mr. Han knows the SINOSURE very well. You'd better contact them in advance.

**Mr. Han:** Don't worry, Mr. Hardaway. I've got an Inquiry Form for Overseas Investment Insurance from SINOSURE already. We can populate the inquiry form with the required information this evening and approach to SINOSURE tomorrow.

## Key Words & Expressions

| | |
|---|---|
| Parable | 比喻 |
| Sovereign guarantee | 主权担保 |
| Fulfill commitments | 兑现承诺 |
| SPV (Special Purpose Vehicle) | 项目公司，特殊目的机构 |
| Full-recourse guarantee | 完全追索权担保 |
| Collateral | 抵押物 |
| Mortgage | 抵押贷款 |
| Limited-recourse guarantee | 有限追索权担保 |
| Completion guarantee | 完工担保 |
| Cost over-run risk | 成本超支风险 |
| Construction delay risk | 工程延误风险 |
| Reimburse debt | 偿还债务 |
| Debt equity ratio | 股本负债率 |
| Long-term loan | 长期贷款 |
| Grace period | 债务宽限期 |
| Libor | 伦敦同业拆借利率 |
| Libor+400 | 伦敦同业拆借利率上浮400点（4%） |
| Banking consortium | 银团 |
| Syndicated loan | 银团贷款 |
| Financial institution | 金融机构 |
| Specific terms of the financing agreement | 融资协议的具体条款 |
| Financing close | 融资关闭 |
| Letter of Intention | 意向函 |
| Risk rating | 风险评级 |
| Inquiry Form for Overseas Investment Insurance | 海外投资保险查询单 |
| SINOSURE (China Export & Credit Insurance Corporation) | 中国出口信用保险公司 |

# 第 9 课　寻求项目融资

## 对话

**韩先生 - M 集团国际承包公司的首席财务官**
**郑先生 - 中国知名商业银行全球金融部总经理**
**Hardaway 先生 - A 国财政部国务秘书**

**韩先生**：郑先生，早上好。

**郑先生**：韩先生，早上好。什么风把你吹来啦？而且为什么跟我不说普通话而说英语啊？

**韩先生**：今天我是和我的 A 国朋友一起来的。这位是 A 国财政部的国务秘书 Hardway 先生。

**郑先生**：幸会，Hardaway 先生。欢迎你光临本行。啊哈，韩先生，我猜你一定又有新项目啦。

**韩先生**：知我者还是郑先生您啊。我们公司打算开发 A 国的东西高速公路。可行性研究已获该国内阁批准。Hardaway 先生和我来这里就是探讨贵行是否可能参与为该项目提供融资的。

**郑先生**：噢，我知道 A 国。Hardaway 先生，贵国是本行正密切关注的 H 洲一颗冉冉升起的星星啊。

**Hardaway 先生**：我很高兴您了解我的国家，非常感激。我认为我们国家就是一只振翅待飞的雄鹰，就盼着上升的气流，那即融资。

**郑先生**：Hardaway 先生，您刚才作了一个恰当而美妙的比喻，我完全赞同。可以让我知道该项目的合同总额和实施模式吗？你们考虑的是融资加设计、采购、施工的模式吗？

**韩先生**：不是的，郑先生。这是一个合同总额约 48 亿美元的建设–运营–移交项目。

**郑先生**：这的确是一个超大项目。你认为该国政府会为这个项目提供主权担保吗？

**Hardaway 先生**：很遗憾，郑先生。我国政府没能力为这一项目的融资提供主权担保。在签署新的主权担保之前，我们必须首先兑现先前主权担保的承诺。

**韩先生**：Hardaway 先生说的全是实情。因此我们计划在当地设立一个项目公司并在其名下提供融资担保。

**郑先生**：就一个商业项目而言，我必须说由一个项目公司开担保是不够的；我认为还是由你们公司为项目提供一个完全追索权担保为好。

**韩先生**：根据我们的财务指导方针，我们公司无论如何不能提供完全追索权担保。

**郑先生：** 那么这个项目公司能提供什么样的抵押物呢？你该明白，不靠主权担保，你们就进入一种抵押贷款的模式。

**韩先生：** 哦，我明白。我们打算以东西高速公路的预期收益作抵押。我们的可行性研究表明内部收益率将达12%以上，这个项目能产生实实在在的现金流和可观的利润。

**郑先生：** 如果内部收益率的预测是可靠的话，这听起来还可以接受。

**Hardaway 先生：** 我们政府承诺了在项目达到盈亏平衡点之前会给项目公司以补偿。

**郑先生：** 假若这样，韩先生，我们的银行将考虑作个妥协，接受有限追索权担保来覆盖成本超支风险、施工延误风险。一旦项目公司不能如期完成项目，你们公司就有责任替项目公司偿还债务。

**韩先生：** 这听起来更为合理一点了。

**郑先生：** 顺便问一下，你能确认一下这个项目的融资结构吗？

**韩先生：** 这个项目眼下是按75/25债股比的传统项目融资结构安排的。也就是25%的投资来自于我们公司，剩余的75%要从金融机构来融资。我们将为这个项目争取15年的长期贷款加5年宽限期。

**Hardaway 先生：** 我想知道你能为这样的项目提供怎样的利率呢？

**郑先生：** 当下我们给基础设施的利率是伦敦同业拆借利率上浮400点。

**韩先生：** 我则是更关心你们银行是否会提供我们所需的全部贷款？

郑先生：我行有兴趣为你们的东西高速公路项目提供贷款。然而因为这个项目巨大而且贷款期长，我觉得只有靠银团来支持了。

Hardaway 先生：你的意思是你建议使用一个银团贷款吗？

郑先生：你说得对。我行担任牵头行，并寻找一些其他的银行和金融机构共同为这个项目提供贷款。

Hardaway 先生：郑先生，你真帮了大忙了！

韩先生：郑先生，您能不能给我发一封确认函，确认您有兴趣参与为东西高速公路项目提供融资。

郑先生：好的，今天下午我就开具融资兴趣函。

Hardaway 先生：你预计从开具融资兴趣函到融资关闭要多长时间啊？

郑先生：通常要 8 到 10 个月。

Hardaway 先生：这似乎是很长的一段时间。我国的内阁正等着提供融资的承诺以便启动特许经营协议的谈判。

郑先生：一旦我们就融资协议的关键条款达成共识，本行会出具一份融资意向函的。

韩先生：我们希望还是快点讨论融资协议的具体条款吧。

郑先生：好，我们下周就能开始讨论细节。哦，我可以提一个重要的事情吗？本行提供海外融资的一个先决条件是要有与该国风险评级相对应的海外投资保险，覆盖政治动乱、外汇限制、没收、毁灭、战争等风险。

Hardaway 先生：谢谢你的提醒。你能给我们介绍一家处理此类业务的保险公司吗？

**郑先生：**中国出口信用保险公司，韩先生对它非常了解。你们还是提前接洽他们为好。

**韩先生：**Hardaway 先生，别担心。我已经从中国出口信用保险公司拿了一份海外投资保险的询保单。我们可以今晚填好询保单所需的信息，明天就去中国出口信用保险公司。

# LESSON 10　NEGOTIATIONS ON THE PROJECT CONCESSION AGREEMENT

**Dialogue**

**Mr. Huang-Vice President of International Contracting Company of Group M**

**Mr. Chen-Director of Commercial Department of International Contracting Company of Group M**

**Mr. Antonio-Vice Minister, Ministry of Infrastructure Development**

**Mr. Harold-Director of Road Department of Ministry of Infrastructure Development**

**Mr. Huang:** Good morning, honorable vice minister. As your request we are here to discuss the project Concession Agreement.

## CHAPTER II PRE-CONTRACT ACTIVITIES OF BOT PROJECT

**Mr. Antonio:** Welcome, Mr. Huang. Have you read the exposure draft of the Concession Agreement prepared by our ministry?

**Mr. Huang:** Yes, of course. It is well structured in the internationally prevalent template of concession agreements. It deals with all the core issues such as concession period, obligations of both the concessionaire and Ministry of Infrastructure Development, the levy and collection of fees, change of law, force majeure, default and termination events, dispute resolution, etc.

**Mr. Antonio:** Oh, you have read our exposure draft quite carefully. Our ministry really worked very hard on this draft. We tried to allocate risk fairly and set out clearly the performance obligations of the principal parties. The objective of the concession agreement is to help securing a reasonable return of investment and to provide efficient and cost-effective services to the West-east Highway users.

**Mr. Huang:** Mr. Antonio, we are sharing these common principles and objectives.

**Mr. Antonio:** Do you have any amendments or comments on our draft concession agreement, which you would like us to consider?

**Mr. Huang:** We do have some suggestions. I'd like to ask Mr. Chen, the Commercial Department Director of our company, to present them.

**Mr. Chen:** Honorable Vice Minister, it is my privilege to meet with you today. We have five suggestions as follows. Firstly, we think some important information should be compiled into Concession Agreement as attachments. This information includes project site locations, site delivery schedule, technical requirements, operation and maintenance requirements, takeover procedure, financing structure, cash flow projection, government support agreement, etc.

**Mr. Antonio:** You are right, Mr. Chen. We didn't have enough time to prepare the attachments. The ministry hopes that your company could help to draft these attachments later on.

**Mr. Huang:** No problem, vice minister. We will draft a set of attachments for your review within ten days.

**Mr. Antonio:** That's fine. I would like to remind you that the technical parameters in the attachments should focus on the 'what' rather than the 'how' in relation to the level of services delivered by the Concessionaire.

**Mr. Chen:** Okay, honorable vice minister. We will follow your instruction in drafting the attachments. Secondly, we suggest simply merging 5 years' construction period and 25 years' O&M period into 30 years' concession period. It means …

**Mr. Harold:** I understand and agree with your intention. I believe that the inclusion of construction period in the concession period will incentivize early completion of the highway, and thus generate greater toll revenues.

**Mr. Huang:** And if there is any delay in the government handing over the possession of the land required, we suggest the concession period should be extended accordingly.

**Mr. Antonio:** I agree, Mr. Huang. Go ahead, Mr. Chen.

**Mr. Chen:** The third suggestion is that the Concession Agreement prohibits competing road construction, including highway, railway or upgrading the parallel existing road which can divert revenue streams away from this project.

**Mr. Harold:** That seems reasonable. But in the scenario where the traffic flow rate exceeds the maximum designed index, the government should have the right to upgrade the existing highway or take any necessary measures to ease the traffic pressure.

**Mr. Huang:** I can't agree with you, Mr. Harold. As you should be aware, designed into the West-east Highway proposal there are two additional lanes being reserved for future expansion in case of excess traffic intensity.

**Mr. Antonio:** All right! I can accept your proposal with respect to competing road construction. However, owing to the absence of an alternative road, the West-east Highway should be opened to local residents to use without any payment of tolls until free service lanes are provided. This would ensure local support for the project and avoid legal challenges or local opposition arising out of easement rights.

**Mr. Huang:** We have no objection on that, honorable vice minister.

**Mr. Chen:** The fourth suggestion is that the Concession Agreement should set out the compensation mechanism for low traffic flow rate.

**Mr. Antonio:** Compensation?

**Mr. Huang:** Oh, vice minister, may I remind you that the Minister has agreed to compensate my company when the traffic flow rate is below the break-even point.

**Mr. Antonio:** I remember that, but our ministry proposes the compensation is provided in the form of concession period extension instead of cash. The ministry agrees an extension of the concession period in the event of a lower than expected traffic growth. Conversely, you will agree that the concession period shall be reduced if the traffic growth exceeds the expected level.

**Mr. Huang:** That compensation mechanism seems equitable and is acceptable for our company.

**Mr. Chen:** The last one we suggest is to have an indexation of the toll rate linked to CPI, and accordingly the toll can be adjusted on an annual basis according to your country's inflation.

**Mr. Antonio:** It is acceptable that the toll rate is linked with the CPI published by the National Bureau of Statistics.

**Mr. Harold:** In confidence may I tell you that the Toll Road Act regulating the entire toll road nationwide is ready to be published soon, this includes detailed provisions regarding the adjustment of toll rate in the way you described.

**Mr. Huang:** Okay, our project will just follow the law.

**Mr. Antonio:** Mr. Harold, please make a hard copy of the draft Toll Road Act for Mr. Huang's reference after the meeting. Oh, by the way, you'd better also make a hard copy of the Law of Private Investment published last year, where Mr. Huang could find all the detailed preferential policies and tax exemptions.

**Mr. Harold:** Okay, I will arrange it.

**Mr. Huang:** Thank you, vice minister.

**Mr. Harold:** Vice minister, since we have discussed all the issues raised by the concessionaire, perhaps we can take this opportunity to confirm outlines of highway maintenance during the concession period.

**Mr. Huang:** In outline we plan to have an overhaul of the highway every five years and minor repairs to be undertaken every two years. We will specify all the details to be included in an attachment entitled

Operation & Maintenance Requirements.

**Mr. Antonio:** Okay. Before our meeting closes, I'd like to touch on two important issues. The first is that we want the monitoring and supervision of construction, operation and maintenance to be undertaken by an independent engineer selected by the government through a transparent process. The engineers' independence would provide added comfort to all stakeholders, besides improving the efficiency of project operations. The second is that in order to enhance security to the lenders and ensure stability to the project operations, all financial inflows and outflows of the project have to be routed through an escrow account.

**Mr. Huang:** We have no objection, honorable vice minister.

**Mr. Antonio:** We hope to sign the Concession Agreement within one month. I will ask the minister to decide the date.

## Key Words & Expressions

| | |
|---|---|
| Concession Agreement | 特许经营权协议 |
| Exposure draft | 征求意见稿 |
| Common principles and objectives | 共同的原则和目标 |
| Cash flow projection | 现金流预测 |
| Technical parameters | 技术参数 |
| Revenue streams | 收入来源 |
| Competing road construction | 竞争性道路的建设 |
| Maximum designed index | 最高的设计指标 |
| Free service lanes | 免费便道 |
| Easement right | 地役权 |
| Compensation mechanism | 补偿机制 |
| Break-even point | 盈亏平衡点 |

| | |
|---|---|
| Indexation of the toll rate | 过路费率指数化 |
| CPI (Consumer Price Index) | 消费物价指数 |
| Toll Road Act | 收费公路法案 |
| Law of Private Investment | 私人投资法 |
| Overhaul | 大修 |
| Minor repairs | 小修 |
| Stakeholders | 利益相关者，干系人 |
| Financial inflows and outflows | 资金的流入和流出 |
| Escrow account | 第三方保管账户 |

# 第10课　项目特许经营权协议谈判

## 对话

黄先生 - M 集团国际承包公司副总裁

陈先生 - M 集团国际承包公司商务部经理

Antonio 先生 - 基础设施建设部副部长

Harold 先生 - 基础设施建设部公路司司长

**黄先生**：尊敬的副部长，早上好！我们是按您的要求来讨论项目的特许经营权协议的。

**Antonio 先生**：欢迎黄先生！你看了我们部准备的特许经营权协议的征求意见稿了吗？

**黄先生**：是的，当然看了。征求意见稿按国际通行的特许经营权协议模板构架得非常好，几乎将所有核心要点都阐述到了，诸如特许经营期、特许权受让人和基础设施建设部双方的义务、征税和收费、法律的改变、不可抗力、违约事件与解约、争议解决等等。

**Antonio 先生：**噢，你对我们的征求意见稿看得很仔细啊。我们部确实在这份征求意见稿上下了大功夫。我们试图做到各主要参与方之间风险分配的公平均衡及义务的对称。其目的就是保障合理的投资回报，并向东西高速公路的用户提供高效率、高性价比的服务。

**黄先生：**Antonio 先生，我们有着共同的原则和目标。

**Antonio 先生：**你对我们的征求意见稿有什么补充和意见需要我们考虑的吗？

**黄先生：**我们的确有几个建议。我想让我公司的商务部经理陈先生来汇报我们的建议。

**陈先生：**尊敬的副部长，我很荣幸今天能与您见面。我们有下列五个建议。首先，我们认为一些重要信息应作为附件编入特许经营权协议，诸如项目现场位置、现场提供计划、技术要求、运维要求、移交程序、融资结构、资金流量预测以及政府支持协议等等。

**Antonio 先生：**对的，陈先生。我们没有时间准备附件了。基础设施建设部希望贵公司随后能帮助编制这些附件。

**黄先生：**没问题，副部长。我们将在 10 天之内草拟一套附件给您审核。

**Antonio 先生：**很好！我想提醒你们有关特许经营权受让者提供的服务水平，在附件的技术参数上应聚焦于"要什么"上，而不是"如何做"上面。

陈先生：好的，尊敬的副部长。我们会按您的指示来起草附件的。其次，我们建议把5年施工期和25年的运营维保期简单合并为30年特许经营期。这个意思是……

Harold 先生：我理解并赞同你的意见。我相信把施工期并入特许经营期将有助于激励公路提前完工，并产生更多的过路费收入。

黄先生：另外，如果政府移交所需土地延误了的话，我们建议特许经营期也应该相应延长。

Antonio 先生：黄先生，我同意。陈先生接着讲吧。

陈先生：第三，我们建议特许经营权协议应明确禁止与之竞争的道路的建设，包括公路、铁路或者与之平行道路的升级，那会分流项目的收入来源。

Harold 先生：这个意见看上去是合理的。不过在交通流率超过最高设计指标的情况下，政府应该有权对现有道路作升级或采取任何措施来缓解交通压力。

黄先生：Harold 先生，我不能同意您的意见。您应该知道，东西高速公路的建议书的设计中已经预留了两个车道供交通强度超限时作扩建的呀。

Antonio 先生：好的，我同意你们关于竞争性道路建设的意见。但是，因为没有可作替代的道路，在提供免费便道之前，东西高速公路应向当地居民开放使用而不收取过路费。这将保证项目获得当地支持并避免因地役权引起的司法挑战或当地的反对。

黄先生：副部长，我们对此没有反对意见。

陈先生：第四，特许经营权协议应给出针对交通流率的补偿机制。

**Antonio 先生**：补偿？

**黄先生**：噢，副部长，我想提醒您，部长答应过当交通流率低于盈亏平衡点的情况下给予我司补偿的。

**Antonio 先生**：我记得，不过我们部建议是以延长特许经营期的形式做补偿，而不是现金的形式。基础设施建设部同意当交通增长低于预期的情况下延长特许经营期。反之，你们须同意当交通增长超过预期水平则缩短特许经营期。

**黄先生**：这样的补偿机制似乎是公平的，我公司可以接受。

**陈先生**：最后一点，我们建议过路费率与消费物价指数挂钩实现指标化，这就可以根据贵国的通胀每年调整过路费。

**Antonio 先生**：将过路费率与国家统计局发布的消费物价指数挂钩没问题。

**Harold 先生**：我想透一点风，规范全国范围内收费公路的收费公路法案即将颁布了，那里有包括你所说的调整过路费率的具体规定。

**黄先生**：那好，我们项目就依法行事。

**Antonio 先生**：Harold 先生，请你会后提供一份拟就的收费公路法案纸质版给黄先生作参考。噢，你最好顺便再弄一份去年颁布的私人投资法的纸质版，黄先生可以在那里找到所有详细的优惠政策和税务减免。

**Harold 先生**：好的，我会安排的。

**黄先生**：谢谢您，副部长。

**Harold 先生**：副部长，既然我们已经讨论了特许经营权受让人提出的所有议题，我想借此机会确认一下高速公路运行期间维护保养的纲要。

**黄先生**：概括地说，我们计划每五年做一次大修，每两年做一次小修。我们会在附件的"运维要求"里作详细的规定。

**Antonio 先生**：好的。在会议结束之前，我想强调两个重要事项。第一个是对建设、运营、维护的监督与管理，必须由政府通过透明的过程遴选出来的独立工程师来承担。除了提升项目运作的效率之外，其独立性还将给所有利益相关方增加舒适感。第二，为了让贷款方增强安全感并确保项目运作的稳定性，所有资金的流入和流出必须通过第三方保管账户。

**黄先生**：尊敬的副部长，我们对此没有异议。

**Antonio 先生**：我们希望在一个月之内签署这份特许经营权协议。我会请部长决定具体日期。

# CHAPTER III   CONTRACT IMPLEMENTATION OF BOT PROJECT

LOCAL REGISTRATION OF THE PROJECT COMPANY
LAND ACQUISITION FOR THE PROJECT
ARRANGING STONE QUARRIES FOR THE PROJECT
IMPORTING HEAVY MACHINERY FROM CHINA
LOCAL WORKERS RECRUITMENT
PROJECT SECURITY DEPLOYMENTS
FULFILLING SOCIAL RESPONSIBILITIES
WHOLE ROAD OPENING TO TRAFFIC
HIGHWAY OPERATION & MAINTENANCE
HIGHWAY TRANSFER TO THE LOCAL AUTHORITY

## 第三章   BOT 项目合同实施

当地注册项目公司

项目征地

为项目安排采石场

从中国进口重型机械

招募当地工人

项目安防部署

履行社会责任

全线通车

高速路运营与养护

向地方当局移交高速路

# CHAPTER III  CONTRACT IMPLEMENTATION OF BOT PROJECT

## LESSON 11  LOCAL REGISTRATION OF THE PROJECT COMPANY

### Dialogue 1

**Mr. Fang-Deputy Project Manager of West-east Highway Project**

**Dr. Lawrence-Director of Investment Authority**

**Mr. Fang:** Excuse me. I am Robert Fang of Group M from China. Is it possible to meet Dr. Lawrence, the director of investment authority?

**Dr. Lawrence:** What do you want to speak to him about?

**Mr. Fang:** Our Group has reached a concession agreement with your Government to develop the West-east Highway on BOT basis. We are going to register a SPV company locally for this project.

**Dr. Lawrence:** I am Doctor Lawrence. I am very pleased to help you in this regard. Can you show me the Concession Agreement?

**Mr. Fang:** Of course. Here you are. This is a hard copy of the Concession Agreement for you to keep.

**Dr. Lawrence:** Thank you. The Concession Agreement seems to be complete and very constructive. Okay, here is an application form for company registration. You need to complete the form and then submit it to me.

**Mr. Fang:** I see, there is a lot of information required. Name of the applicant, brief background of the applicant, name of the project to be invested, brief description of the project to be invested…

**Dr. Lawrence:** Yes. The most important section is where you provide information relating to the source of your finance for the project, anticipated earnings especially the anticipated foreign currency earnings…

**Mr. Fang:** Yes, of course. The form also requires information on our Employment Scheme, the Importation Scheme for Equipment & Machinery, local materials to be used and in addition you want to know about pollution/waste/hazardous articles that might be produced during the construction activities. We have all these information in our Feasibility Study Report of the project. May I take this form back to my office, complete it and return it within a couple of days?

**Dr. Lawrence:** Of course, you may take it back to your office. I will be waiting for you to submit your application form. If you have any queries regarding this form, please feel free to contact me any time.

## Dialogue 2

**Mr. Fang:** Good morning, Dr. Lawrence. We have completed the application form for company registration. But I am really not sure if we have done it properly. Would it be possible for you to review the Application Form before we formally submit it?

**Dr. Lawrence:** Sure, let me look it over. Well, you have provided the necessary information in detail. Oh, you haven't included the address where the company is to be registered.

**Mr. Fang:** Yes, we didn't fill in the address because we had not decided which city to use for our company registration. We heard that the company registration location can greatly affect the tax regime the company enjoys. Is that correct?

**Dr. Lawrence:** Yes, you are right. We have divided our country into three taxation zones. Zone A includes the capital and some coastal provinces which the economy is relatively more active; Zone C includes the inland remote provinces which the economy is inactive; Zone B includes the other provinces in which the economy is just in the middle. We allocate the highest tax benefits to the companies registered in the provinces of Zone C, the lowest tax benefits to the ones of Zone A, and the middle tax benefits to the ones of Zone B.

**Mr. Fang:** Can you explain to me in more details the differences in tax benefits in different Zones?

**Dr. Lawrence:** Yes, I can. Generally the tax benefits for foreign investors have two dimensions. One dimension is import duty relief, and the other is corporation tax relief. The periods of import duty relief are 3 years, 4 years and 6 years for Zone A, Zone B and Zone C respectively. And the period of corporation tax relief is 8, 12 and 15 years for Zone A, B and C respectively.

**Mr. Fang:** May we register our SPV for the West-east Highway in any of the three Zones?

**Dr. Lawrence:** Yes, you can register your company in any province of this country as you like, whatever in which Zone.

**Mr. Fang:** Since the West-east Highway will cross the provinces in all the Zones A, B and C, in consideration of the difference of tax benefits in the three Zones, it makes financial sense to register our company in a province of Zone C. But I am hesitant about that because it might cause communication inconvenience between the SPV company and the Ministry of Infrastructure Development.

**Dr. Lawrence:** Don't worry too much about that. You can register your company in a remote province of Zone C and set up a branch office in the capital to help keep a close relationship with the ministries.

**Mr. Fang:** Oh, this is a good idea. In this case I will register the SPV in one of the provinces of Zone C. We already have a site office in one of the Zone C provinces. We are using that office for our topographic surveys. May I use that site office address for the registration of the SPV company?

**Dr. Lawrence:** Yes, you can.

**Mr. Fang:** Okay, I can submit the completed application form to you right now. Can you tell me how many days it will be before we will receive your approval?

**Dr. Lawrence:** After my office undertakes a preliminary review, your application form will be submitted to the Joint Review Committee which is made up of multiple ministries for final approval. It usually takes 3 or 4 weeks, but anyway not exceeding the 45 days stipulated.

**Mr. Fang:** The sooner the better. We will be waiting for the Foreign Investment Certificate so that we can apply for our staffs' working visa and open our bank account. You are really helpful! Thank you very much.

## Key-words & Expressions

| | |
|---|---|
| SPV (Special Purpose Vehicle) | 特殊目的机构，项目公司 |
| Application Form | 申请表 |
| Company Registration | 公司注册 |
| Employment Scheme | 雇佣计划 |
| Importation Scheme of Equipment & Machinery | 机械设备进口计划 |
| Pollution/waste/hazardous articles | 污染/废物/危险品 |
| Feasibility Study Report | 可行性研究报告 |
| Tax regime | 税收体制，税收政策 |
| Taxation Zone | 税收区域 |
| Import duty relief | 进口关税减免 |
| Corporation tax relief | 公司所得税减免 |
| Site office | 现场办公室 |
| Joint Review Committee | 联合审查委员会 |
| Foreign Investment Certificate | 外商投资证书 |
| Working visa | 工作签证 |
| Bank account | 银行账户 |

# 第三章　BOT 项目合同实施

## 第 11 课　当地注册项目公司

**对话 1**

**方先生 - 东西高速公路项目副总经理**
**Lawrence 博士 - 投资局局长**

**方先生**：打扰了。我是来自中国的 M 集团的 Robert Fang。我可以见一下投资局局长 Lawrence 博士吗？

**Lawrence 博士**：你想要和他谈什么事情？

**方先生**：我集团已与贵国政府达成以 BOT 方式开发东西高速公路的特许经营权协议。我们打算为这个项目在当地注册一家 SPV 公司。

**Lawrence 博士**：我就是 Lawrence 博士。非常高兴能在这方面帮到您。您可以给我看一下特许经营权协议吗？

**方先生**：当然可以。给您。这是为您准备的特许权经营协议的纸质版。

**Lawrence 博士：** 谢谢你。看来这份特许经营权协议很完整、很有建设性啊。好的，这是公司注册申请表。你需要先填写表格然后提交给我。

**方先生：** 我明白，有很多空格要填啊。申请人姓名、申请人简介、投资项目名称、投资项目简介……

**Lawrence 博士：** 是的。最重要的是那些有关项目的资金来源、预期收益、特别是预期的外汇收入等信息的部分。

**方先生：** 确实是的。表格还需要我们的雇佣计划、机械设备进口计划、需用当地材料的信息，此外你们还要知道施工过程中可能产生的污染/废物/危险物。所有这些信息在我们项目可行性研究报告中都有。我可以把这张表格带回我的办公室、几天内填好了再交来吗？

**Lawrence 博士：** 当然可以，你可以把它带回去。我等着你来提交申请表格。如果你对表格有任何问题，请随时与我联系。

## 对话 2

**方先生：** 早上好，Lawrence 博士。公司注册申请表我们已经填好了。但我真的不敢确定我们填写得是否正确。你能在我们正式提交之前检查一下吗？

**Lawrence 博士：** 当然可以，让我看一下。嗯，你已经详细地提供了必要的信息。哦，你还没有填写公司的注册地址。

**方先生：** 是的，我们没有填写这个地址，因为我们还没有决定在哪个城市注册公司。我们听说公司注册的地点会极大地影响其享有的税务政策，是吗？

**Lawrence 博士**：是的，你说得对。我们把我国领土划分为三类税收区域。A 类区包括首都和经济相对较活跃的沿海省份；C 类区包括经济不活跃的内陆偏远省份；B 类区包括其他经济状况中等的省份。我们对在 C 类区省份注册的公司给予最高的税收优惠，而给 A 类区的最低，B 类区的则处于中间。

**方先生**：您能详细解释一下不同税收区域的税收优惠之间的差异吗？

**Lawrence 博士**：是的，我能给你解释。对外国投资者的税收优惠主要是在两个维度上，一是进口关税减免，二是公司所得税减免。进口关税减免的期限 A 类区、B 类区和 C 类区分别为 3 年、4 年和 6 年。公司所得税减免期限 A 类区、B 类区和 C 类区分别为 8、12 和 15 年。

**方先生**：我们可以在这三个区域中的任何一个注册我们东西高速公路的 SPV 吗？

**Lawrence 博士**：是的，你可以按照你的意愿在这个国家的任何一个省份注册你的公司，无论是在哪个区域。

**方先生**：由于东西高速公路将跨越 A、B、C 三类区域的省份，考虑到这三类区域税收优惠的不同，我们在 C 类区域的省份注册我们的公司经济上是有意义的。但我还是犹豫不定，因为这可能会给 SPV 公司和基础设施建设部之间的沟通带来不便。

**Lawrence 博士**：别担心。你可以在 C 类区域的偏远省份注册你的公司，并在首都设立一个分支机构以便与各部委保持密切联系。

**方先生**：哦，这是个好主意。这样的话，我就在一个 C 类区域的省份注册 SPV 啦。我们在 C 类区域的一个省已经有一个现场办公室，用于我们的地形测量。我可以用这个现场办公室的地址作 SPV 公司注册吗？

**Lawrence 博士：** 是的，你可以。

**方先生：** 好的，我现在就可以把填好的申请表交给你了。你能告诉我多少天之后我们才能收到您的批准吗？

**Lawrence 博士：** 经过我的办公室初步审查后，你们的申请表会提交给由多个部委组成的联合审查委员会作最终批准。通常需要 3 到 4 周，不过至多不超过规定的 45 天。

**方先生：** 越快越好哦！我们还等着用外商投资证书去申请我们员工的工作签证以及开立我们的银行账户呢。您真是帮了大忙了。非常感谢。

# LESSON 12  LAND ACQUISITION FOR THE PROJECT

## Dialogue 1

**Mr. Fang-Deputy General Manager of Project Company**

**Mr. Raphael-Vice Minister of Infrastructure Development Ministry**

**Mr. Fang:** Good Morning, honorable vice minister. Last week our company submitted a letter to your Ministry regarding the possession of the plots of land necessary for the West-east Highway development. I wonder if that letter has been brought to your attention or not.

**Mr. Raphael:** Yes, my secretary handed that letter to me three days ago. I read it and instructed my secretary to forward your letter to all the relevant provincial governments.

**Mr. Fang:** Oh, thank you, honorable vice minister. Then, how long do you think it will be before our teams can occupy the plots and commence construction on the allocated land?

**Mr. Raphael**: Umm, that's a very tough question. You know, land acquisition is a very complicated issue because it involves a lot of private properties, and also arable land which is currently being used to grow crops. I really don't know how long it will take for such a tough issue to be settled. It depends a lot on the provincial governments.

**Mr. Fang**: Honorable vice minister, as we both understand possession of the site is one of the most essential prerequisites for the development of the highway. We submitted our program to your ministry one and half month ago. The program shows the relevant commencement date for each of the plots. The Concession Agreement explicitly stipulates that the State Government shall ensure the land is available for the timely commencement of the construction for the Highway, and the Concession Agreement also specifies that the Infrastructure Development Ministry represents the State Government and has complete authority for this project.

**Mr. Raphael**: Well, Mr. Fang, our ministry will certainly take this responsibility on behalf of State Government seriously. I will organize a series of on-site coordination meetings in the relevant provinces to make sure the land acquisition proceeds in an efficient and timely manner. My secretary will send you a schedule of the on-site coordination meetings within this week.

**Mr. Fang**: Oh, very good. I was getting to be really stressed concerning the progress of this essential matter. Your plan to organize a series of on-site coordination meetings seems to the best way forward. We will make all the necessary data ready for the on-site coordination meetings. Thank you, honorable vice minister.

**Mr. Raphael**: Okay, see you on the coordination meetings soon.

## Dialogue 2

**Mr. Fang-Deputy General Manager of Project Company**

**Mr. Raphael-Vice Minister of Infrastructure Development Ministry**

**Mr. Louis-Vice Province's Governor.**


**Mr. Raphael:** Good morning, vice governor, I believe you have received my letter and you know the purpose of this meeting very well. We'd like to hear the progress of land acquisition for the West-East Highway in your province.

**Mr. Louis:** I am so sorry, vice minister. On the land acquisition, we haven't got any real progress to report yet. If we look at the map you can see, these are the tracts of land to be acquired. Unfortunately it isn't uncultivated land, there are croplands and farm houses within this area. The villagers are looking for a large amount of compensation before they consent to the sale of their land. But the Province Government doesn't have money for such compensation.

**Mr. Raphael:** I fully understand your situation. I have some good news for you. The land acquisition budget for West-east Highway has just been approved by the Cabinet. The money for compensation can be applied for right now.

**Mr. Louis:** That is what we are looking for, vice minister. Do you have application documents?

**Mr. Raphael:** Yes, here you are.

**Mr. Louis:** I see. There is a lot of detailed information required, the number and type of houses, number of rooms in each house, crop species and exact area of land for each villager, number and species of trees.

**Mr. Raphael:** You know we have settled the compensation standard rates for the different types of houses, the different species of crops and trees. Your application needs to apply such standard rates in the calculation of compensation amount.

**Mr. Louis:** Yes, I know. But where can I find such a big team to make the survey in short time?

**Mr. Raphael:** Don't worry, vice governor. Mr. Fang of the project company will help you in this respect.

**Mr. Fang:** Vice governor, I can organize a team of five surveyors with all the necessary instruments to be available starting tomorrow morning, if you can assign a local official who can show us all the corner points of each villager's farm land. Once we are on location and set up, using the RTK instrument our surveyors will record the accurate coordinates of the corner points in minutes, then attach the coordinates on our map. And with our specially developed computer software, we will be able to calculate the exact cropland area for each villager on the same day.

**Mr. Louis:** Really? It sounds fantastic, almost too good to be true. In this case, I will immediately assign one official to work supporting your survey team. I will order him to contact the village heads this afternoon, so that they can set stakes at the corner of each piece of cropland. Please give me your cellphone number. Our official will call you as soon as he gets things organized.

**Mr. Fang:** This is my name card with my cellphone number on it. I will keep my cellphone on all the time and wait for your order to start the survey.

**Mr. Raphael:** We've just had a very productive meeting. Vice governor, I will be waiting for your compensation application then, hopefully within this week.

**Mr. Louis:** Believe me, vice minister. It will be done by the end of this week. You will find our compensation application on your desk next Monday morning.

## Key-words & Expressions

| | |
|---|---|
| Land acquisition | 征地 |
| Possession of the plots (possession of site) | 进入地块（进入现场） |
| Commencement date | 开工日期 |
| On-site coordination meeting | 现场协调会议 |
| Uncultivated land | 荒地，处女地 |
| Croplands | 农田 |
| Farm house | 农舍 |
| Money of compensation | 补偿金 |
| Corner point | 角点 |
| Coordinates | 坐标 |
| RTK (Real-time kinematic) | 实时动态差分技术 |
| RTK instrument | 实时动态差分测量仪器 |
| Too good to be true | 好得难以置信 |

# 第 12 课　项目征地

## 对话 1

**方先生 - 东西高速公路项目副总经理**
**Raphael 先生 - 基础设施建设部副部长**

**方先生**：早上好，尊敬的副部长。上个星期我们公司向贵部提交了一封关于进入东西高速公路开发所需用地块的函件。我想知道您是否已经注意到那封信。

**Raphael 先生**：是的，我的秘书三天前就把那封信交给我了。我读了那封信并指示我的秘书转发给所有相关的省政府。

**方先生**：噢，谢谢您，尊敬的副部长。那么，您认为我们的队伍多久才能占用地块并在指定地块上开始施工呢？

**Raphael 先生**：嗯，那是一个很难回答的问题啊。你知道，土地征用是一个非常复杂的事情，涉及很多私人财产和眼下种着农作物的耕地。我真不知道这么棘手的问题我们需要多久才能解决。这很大程度上取决于各省政府啦。

**方先生**：尊敬的副部长，我们双方都明白进入现场是公路开发的最基本前提之一。我们在一个半月前向贵部提交了我们的计划，说明了每个地块对应的开工日期。特许经营权协议明确规定，贵国政府应确保公路建设的用地到位，以便按时开工；特许经营权协议还指定，基础设施建设部对于该项目代表国家政府并全权负责。

**Raphael 先生**：好吧，方先生，我们部当然会代表国家政府认真地承担这一责任。我将在相关省份组织一系列现场协调会，以确保土地征用工作有效、及时地开展。我的秘书将在本周内把现场协调会的日程安排发给你。

**方先生**：噢，非常好。此前我对这一重要事宜的进程感到非常紧张。您计划安排一系列现场协调会议看来是推进的最好办法。我们将为确保现场协调会准备好所有必要的数据。谢谢您，尊敬的副部长。

**Raphael 先生**：好的，协调会上见。

## 对话 2

**方先生 - 项目公司副总经理**

**Raphael 先生 - 基础设施建设部副部长**

**Louis 先生 - 副省长**

**Raphael 先生**：副省长，早上好。我相信你已经收到了我的函件并很清楚这次会议的目的了。我们想听一听贵省范围内东西高速公路征地的进展情况。

**Louis 先生**：非常抱歉，副部长。我们在征地方面还没有任何实质性进展可汇报。如果我们看看地图，您会看到，这大片的就是需要征用的土地。很遗憾，那可不是荒地啊，这个范围里既有农田又有农舍。在同意出售他们的土地之前，村民们都盼着可观的补偿呢。但省政府可没有钱去支付补偿啊。

**Raphael 先生**：我完全理解你的处境。我有个好消息要告诉你，东西高速公路的征地预算在内阁刚刚通过了。现在就可以申请补偿金了。

**Louis 先生**：那正是我们所需要的，副部长。您有申请材料吗？

**Raphael 先生**：有，给你。需要填写好多详细信息哦，不过我会尽可能地提供帮助的。

**Louis 先生**：我明白。表格需要填写的详细信息可真多啊，每户村民的房屋数量和类型、每座房屋的房间数量、作物种类和确切面积、树木种类和数量。

**Raphael 先生**：你知道我们已经为不同类型的房屋、不同种类的农作物和树木制定了补偿标准。你们的申请可要按这些标准费率来计算补偿金额哦。

**Louis 先生**：是的，我知道。但是在短时间内我从哪里去找这么大一支队伍进行测量啊？

**Raphael 先生**：别担心，副省长。在这方面项目公司的方先生会帮助你的。

**方先生**：副省长，如果您能指派一名当地官员为我们指出每个村民农田的所有角点，我可以组织一个由五名测量员组成的小组，带着所有必要的仪器明天一早就开始工作。一旦我们到位并准备就绪，利用 RTK 设备我们的测量员会在几分钟内就录入角点的精确坐标，然后将坐标标到我们的地图上。借助专门开发的电脑软件，我们当天就能计算出每一户村民农田的确切面积。

**Louis 先生**：真的吗？听起来太不可思议了，好得几乎难以置信。这样的话，我将立即指派一名官员支持你们测量小组的工作。我将命令他今天下午就联系各村村长，那样他们可以在每一块农田的拐角设桩。请告诉我你的手机号码。一旦我们的官员把事情安排妥当就给你打电话。

**方先生**：这是我的名片，上面有我的手机号码。我会保持手机一直开机，等待您开始测量的命令。

**Raphael 先生**：我们刚刚开了一个非常有成效的会议。副省长，那么我就等你的补偿申请啦，希望本周内就能收到。

**Louis 先生**：相信我，副部长。我们会在本周末完成，下周一早上你就会在你的办公桌上看到我们的补偿申请了。

## LESSON 13  ARRANGING STONE QUARRIES FOR THE PROJECT

### Dialogue 1

**Mr. Fang-Deputy General Manager of Project Company**

**Mr. Peng-Chief Engineer of Project Company**

**Mr. Thomson-Director of Provincial Territory & Resource Authority**

**Mr. Fang:** Good Morning, Mr. Thomson. I am ···

**Mr. Thomson:** You are Mr. Fang from the West-east Highway Project Company. I think we met before.

**Mr. Fang:** Yes, I met you at a meeting in Provincial Governor's office. I asked the Provincial Government for support on sourcing aggregates for the construction of West-east Highway Project. You

# CHAPTER III  CONTRACT IMPLEMENTATION OF BOT PROJECT

kindly gave me the names, addresses and contact persons of five major local aggregates suppliers, and advised us to contact them. On behalf of my company, I'd like to express our gratitude to you.

**Mr. Thomson:** Oh, well that's part of my job. Do you believe that those local aggregates suppliers can meet your project requirements?

**Mr. Fang:** Not really. We have undertaken an in-depth investigation of the local aggregates suppliers, but the conclusion of the investigation was not satisfactory. My colleague Mr. Peng, the chief engineer of our project company, will report you in detail.

**Mr. Thomson:** Okay, nice to see you, Mr. Peng.

**Mr. Peng:** Mr. Thomson, this is our investigation report on the five local aggregates suppliers. You can find the aggregates production capacity and product performance indexes of each supplier on page 6 of the investigation report.

**Mr. Thomson:** I see, so this is a summary list of the suppliers production capacity.

**Mr. Peng:** Bearing in mind the scale of the West-east Highway Project, the capacity of each of the local aggregates supplier is quite limited, less than 150 cubic meters per day, and even with a combined total production capacity of about 600 cubic meters per day. This is far below our anticipated aggregates demand for the project.

**Mr. Thomson:** Can you tell me the anticipated daily aggregates demand of your project?

**Mr. Peng:** According to the calculation based on the length of the highway within your province and the Master Program, we estimate that the average aggregates supply in your province needs about 4,500 cubic meters each day.

**Mr. Thomson**: That's huge. Do you think your project company can help the local suppliers to increase their production capacity?

**Mr. Fang**: If the difference was not too big, I think our company would be able to help them raising their production capacity to meet the project aggregates demand. But we feel that the gap between the local supply capacity and the project demands is simply too big.

**Mr. Peng**: Another very critical issue is the quality of the aggregates. The performance indexes of the aggregates from those local suppliers does not fully meet the specification requirements of a high-grade highway.

**Mr. Thomson**: Really? Can you show me the evidence of this?

**Mr. Peng**: Yes, of course. In our Investigation Report we have included the test reports on the aggregates samples provided by the five local suppliers. The Report shows that samples from four of the five suppliers meet the technical requirements for the highway sub-base and upper-base, but only one sample meets the technical requirements for the pavement.

**Mr. Thomson**: What are the specifications requirements that make most of the aggregates from our local suppliers unqualified?

**Mr. Peng**: The Crush Index and Los Angeles Abrasion Rate for aggregates to be used in pavements are much more demanding than the ones in base courses. This is because the pavements must be able to directly withstand all the dynamic loads imposed both vertically and horizontally.

**Mr. Thomson**: In this case, do you have a proposal for aggregates

# CHAPTER III  CONTRACT IMPLEMENTATION OF BOT PROJECT

supply?

**Mr. Fang:** We would like to invest in a new stone quarry in this province so that it can be the main source of qualitative aggregates for the highway. It is still our intention to enter into contracts to purchase the aggregates from the local suppliers as a supplementary source.

**Mr. Thomson:** We have some potential quarry sites in the mountainous region; you can see the locations of the quarry sites on this map. But you should be aware that the access conditions are pretty terrible.

**Mr. Fang:** Please allow us to investigate the quarry sites and collect rock samples for analysis first. If the tests show the aggregates meet all the requirements for the West-east Highway, we will build a haul road to facilitate access. After all, building roads is our business.

**Mr. Thomson:** Okay, I will take you to the potential quarry sites next Monday.

**Mr. Fang:** Oh, thank you. We will drive our jeep and pick you up from this office at seven o'clock next Monday morning.


**Dialogue 2**


**Mr. Wang-Manager of Quarry**

**Mr. Xu-Safety Officer of Quarry**

**Mr. Robert-Inspector of Explosive Control Office**

**Mr. Robert:** A month ago our office received your application to acquire, store and use explosives. As explosives are very dangerous and have to be treated carefully, we gave your company a copy of Control Regulations for Explosives together with an Instruction Manual which covers our requirements related to the use of explosives. Your company has been requested to take all the necessary measures in accordance with the Instruction Manual.

**Mr. Wang:** Yes, we have received a copy of the Regulations and the Manual. We understand that access to and the use of explosives are very sensitive, and we have been working hard to ensure that our systems fully comply with or exceed the requirements set out in the Regulations and the Instruction Manual.

**Mr. Robert:** Well, I am glad to hear that. I am here to check up your preparations to ensure compliance both in terms of control systems and site facilities for the safe storage and movement of explosives.

**Mr. Wang:** This is a chart which illustrates our control system for explosives.

**Mr. Robert:** Who is the technical officer responsible for the control of explosives in your quarry?

**Mr. Xu:** It's me. I am the safety officer for the quarry. This is my certificate which confirms that I am qualified in the safe handling and safe use of explosives.

**Mr. Robert:** How many qualified blasters do you have?

**Mr. Xu:** We have five qualified blasters. All of them have obtained their qualification certificates in China. Here are the blaster qualification certificates together with notarized translations.

**Mr. Robert:** Have you built the storage facility for explosives?

**Mr. Xu:** Yes, the explosives' magazines have been built strictly according to the Instruction Manual.

**Mr. Robert:** Let's check it up on site.

**Mr. Song:** Our explosives' magazines are built at the bottom of two small hills. You can see that is surrounded by hills on the three sides and leaves an access only from the front towards the road. We chose this location as the best one so as to prevent any unauthorized access to the explosives' magazines.

**Mr. Robert:** You have selected the right location.

**Mr. Xu:** The perimeter of the explosives' storage facility is fully enclosed with 2 meters high masonry wall in the front and barbed fencing along the bottom of the hills.

**Mr. Robert:** Where is the guard room for the explosives' storage facility?

**Mr. Xu:** That is at the right corner of the front wall. And you see, this part of fencing wall is built of reinforced concrete instead of brick in accordance with the Instruction Manual.

**Mr. Robert:** Good. Then let me check your magazines.

**Mr. Xu:** We have built two magazines here, one for powder and another for detonators with 15 meters' separation in between.

**Mr. Robert:** I see you have set up hazard warning signs in both English and Chinese language at all notable locations. I'd like to take some photos for my report. Please send me all the relevant files you are required to submit, I will include them in my report. If you get me that information by tomorrow, and based on what I have seen today, I believe that your company will have your license for using explosives within ten days.

## Key-words & Expressions

| | |
|---|---|
| Aggregates supply | 骨料供应 |
| Investigation Report | 调查报告 |
| Summary List of Production Capacity | 产能一览表 |
| Bearing in mind | 记住,考虑到 |
| Performance indexes | 性能指标 |
| Sub-base | 底基层 |
| Upper-base | 上基层 |
| Crush Index | 压碎指数 |
| Los Angeles Abrasion Rate | 洛杉矶磨损率 |
| Dynamic loads | 动荷载 |
| Stone quarry | 采石场 |
| Explosives | 爆炸品 |
| Explosive Control Regulation | 爆炸品控制条例 |
| Instruction Manual | 说明书 |
| Safety officer | 安全员 |
| Blaster | 爆破工 |
| Notarization | 公证 |
| Magazines | 爆炸品仓库 |
| Barbed fencing | 带尖刺的栅栏 |
| Reinforced concrete | 钢筋混凝土 |
| Detonator | 雷管 |
| Hazard warning signs | 危险警告标志 |

# 第 13 课　为项目安排采石场

## 对话 1

**方先生 - 项目公司副总经理**
**彭先生 - 项目公司总工程师**
**Thomson 先生 - 省国土资源局局长**

**方先生：**早上好，Thomson 先生。我是……

**Thomson 先生：**你是东西高速公路项目公司的方先生。我想我们之前见过。

**方先生：**是的，我在省长办公室开会时见过您。我请求省政府为东西高速公路项目建设提供骨料资源方面的支持。您和善地给了我当地五大骨料供应商的名称、地址和联系人，并建议我们联系他们。我谨代表我公司向您表达我们的谢意。

**Thomson 先生：**哦，那是我工作的一部分。你觉得那些当地的骨料供应商能满足你们的需要吗?

**方先生**：不见得能满足啊。我们对那些当地的骨料供应商进行了深入的调查，但调查的结论并不令人满意。我的同事彭先生，我们项目公司的总工程师，将会向您作详细汇报。

**Thomson 先生**：好的，很高兴见到你，彭先生。

**彭先生**：Thomson 先生，这是我们对当地五家供应商的调查报告。在调查报告的第 6 页您可以找到每家供应商的骨料生产能力和产品性能指标。

**Thomson 先生**：我明白，这是供应商产能一览表。

**彭先生**：考虑到东西高速公路项目的规模，当地每个骨料供应商的生产能力都相当有限，每天不到 150 立方米，即使合并在一起总生产能力每天大约 600 立方米。那远远达不到我们项目期望的骨料需求。

**Thomson 先生**：你能告诉我你们项目每天的骨料需用量吗?

**彭先生**：根据你们省内的公路长度和总进度计划来计算，本省骨料的日平均供应量大约需要 4500 立方米。

**Thomson 先生**：那是巨大的用量。你认为你们的项目公司能帮助那些当地供应商提高生产能力吗?

**方先生**：如果差距不太大，我想我们公司可以帮助他们提高生产能力来满足项目的骨料需求。但我们觉得当地供应能力与项目需求之间的差距简直太大了。

**彭先生**：另一个非常关键的问题是骨料的质量。当地供应商的骨料性能指标不能完全满足高等级公路技术说明书的要求。

**Thomson 先生**：真的吗? 你能给我看看证据吗?

**彭先生**：好的，当然可以。我们的调查报告中已经包含了当地五个供应商提供的骨料样品的检测报告。报告显示，五个样本中有四个符合公路底基层和上基层的技术要求，但符合路面的技术要求的只有一个样本。

**Thomson 先生**：什么技术说明书的要求让我们大部分本地供应商提供的骨料都不合格呢？

**彭先生**：路面铺设对于骨料的压碎指数和洛杉矶磨损率的要求比基层要高得多，因为路面必须能直接承受垂直和水平方向施加的动荷载。

**Thomson 先生**：这样的话，你们对骨料供应有什么建议吗？

**方先生**：我们想在贵省投资一座新的采石场，以便作为高速公路符合质量要求的主要骨料来源；我们仍打算与本地供应商签约采购骨料以作为补充。

**Thomson 先生**：我们在山区有一些潜在的采石矿点；你可以在这张地图上看到矿点的位置。可是你们得知道那里的进场条件非常糟糕。

**方先生**：请允许我们先踏勘一下采石矿点并采集岩样进行分析。如果试验结果表明该处的骨料达到了东西高速公路的所有要求，那么我们将修建一条运输道路便于通行。毕竟，修路是我们的事情。

**Thomson 先生**：那好，下周一我会带你们去潜在的采石矿点。

**方先生**：哦，谢谢。下周一早上 7 点我们会开吉普车来这个办公室接您。

## 对话 2

王先生 - 采石场经理

许先生 - 采石场安全员

**Robert 先生** - 爆炸物管控办公室检察员

**Robert 先生**：我们办公室一个月前收到了你们关于获取、储存并使用爆炸品的申请。因为爆炸品非常危险，必须要谨慎处理，我们给了贵公司一份《爆炸品控制条例》和一本包括有关爆炸品使用各个方面的《指引手册》，要求贵公司按照《指引手册》采取一切必要措施。

**王先生**：是的，我们已经收到了《条例》和《指引手册》。我们明白接近和使用爆炸品是非常敏感的，我们一直在努力工作以确保我们的体系完全符合或者超过《条例》和《指引手册》所规定的要求。

**Robert 先生**：好的，听你这么说我很高兴。我来这里就是要检查一下你们的准备工作，以确保爆炸品的安全存放与移动在控制体系和现场设施两方面都符合要求。

**王先生**：这是我们的爆炸品控制体系的示意图。

**Robert 先生**：你们采石场负责爆炸品控制的技术人员是谁？

**许先生**：是我。我是采石场的安全员。这是我证明我在爆炸品安全处置和安全使用方面合格的证书。

**Robert 先生**：你们有多少合格的爆破工？

**许先生**：我们有五名合格的爆破工。他们在中国都取得了资质证书。这是他们的资质证书和经过公证的翻译件。

**Robert 先生：** 你们建好爆炸品仓库了吗？

**许先生：** 是的，爆炸品仓库是严格按照手册建造的。

**Robert 先生：** 我们去现场检查一下吧。

**王先生：** 我们的爆炸品仓库建在两座小山的山脚下，三面有山围绕，只有在朝向公路的正面留了入口。我们选择这里作为最佳位置，以防止任何人未经授权进入爆炸品仓库。

**Robert 先生：** 你们选对了地方。

**许先生：** 爆炸品仓库设施的周边已经完全封闭起来，前面是两米高的砌体墙，山脚下则是铁丝网围栏。

**Robert 先生：** 爆炸品仓库设施的警卫室在哪里？

**许先生：** 在正面围墙的右角。你看，这段围墙是按照《指引手册》用钢筋混凝土建造的，而不是用砖砌的。

**Robert 先生：** 很好。那么让我检查一下你们的爆炸品仓库。

**许先生：** 我们在这里建造了两座爆炸品仓库，一个装炸药，另一个装雷管，中间留了 15 米间隔。

**Robert 先生：** 我看到你们在一些醒目的位置竖了中英文危险警示标志。我想为我的报告拍些照片。请你们把所有需要提交的相关文件发给我，我会把它们纳入我的报告。如果你们明天能把那些资料给我的话，基于我今天看到的情况，我相信十天之内你们公司就会拿到爆炸品使用许可证了。

# LESSON 14  IMPORTING HEAVY MACHINERY FROM CHINA

**Dialogue 1**

**Mr. Fang-Deputy General Manager of Project Company**

**Mr. Smith-Deputy Director of Port Authority**

**Mr. Hamilton-Shipping Agent**

**Mr. Fang:** I am deputy general manager of West-east Highway Project Company. This is my name card. And this is our shipping agent Mr. Hamilton. Since West-east Highway Project needs a great deal of machinery and material importation urgently, Mr. Renal, vice minister of Infrastructure Development Ministry advised me to meet you.

**Mr. Smith:** Welcome, Mr. Fang and Mr. Hamilton. Mr. Renal informed me your visit yesterday. What kind of machinery are you going to import?

**Mr. Fang:** Mainly road and bridge construction machinery, including large earth-moving plants, rollers, asphalt pavers, pile drivers, special machines for bridge construction and etc.

**Mr. Smith:** What is approximate total amount of your machinery importation?

**Mr. Fang:** Oh, that's too much. Regarding heavy construction machinery, around 400 sets need to be imported. Taking medium and small plants and equipment into account, the amount will exceed 1,500 sets.

**Mr. Smith:** That is a big amount. What can I help you then?

**Mr. Hamilton:** Could you show us around your port and introduce the relative facilities? We have to investigate the basic conditions of the discharging port before placing a vessel order.

**Mr. Smith:** My pleasure. Let's go around the port together. You can see the docks are in the front along the sea shore.

**Mr. Fang:** What is the total piers length of your port?

**Mr. Smith:** The total length of shoreline is about 1 km. On the left, there is the terminal for general and bulk cargo which occupies around 550m, and on the right, for containers 400m more.

**Mr. Fang:** How many berths all together?

**Mr. Smith:** There are totally five berths, three on the left and two on the right. According to your machinery to be imported, I think you need to order a bulk cargo vessel rather than container one.

**Mr. Hamilton:** Sure, we will order bulk cargo vessel. What is the depth of the berths and the access channel? And what is the maximum size of vessel accessible?

**Mr. Smith:** The berths for general and bulk cargo have a depth of 10m, and for containers 11m. The depth of access channel is more than 13m. 50,000-tonnage is the maximum size of vessel being able to berth in our port.

**Mr. Hamilton:** I have not seen big shore cranes here? Do you have enough cranes for unloading the vessels?

**Mr. Smith:** We have only two shore cranes, one for general and bulk cargo and another for containers. But nowadays, the shore crane for general and bulk cargo is under repair. We are using floating crane to unload the vessels.

**Mr. Hamilton:** In this case, the unloading rate will be severely affected. Mr. Fang, I think we have to order a vessel with its own ship crane then.

**Mr. Smith:** Yes, I strongly suggest you order a vessel with ship crane to ensure the unloading rate.

## Dialogue 2

**Mr. Qiu-Materials & Logistics Manager of Project Company**

**Mr. Masson-Customs Officer**

**Mr. Henry-Customs Broker**

**Mr. Qiu:** Good morning, sir. We are from West-east Highway Project Company. All of our cargo has been moved into customs supervision warehouse area. May we go through the customs clearance formalities here?

**Mr. Masson:** Yes, of course. Please show me your shipment documents.

**Mr. Henry:** Here you are. These are our OBL ( ocean bill of lading ), Packing List and Invoices.

**Mr. Masson:** Have you made commodity inspection at the loading port?

**Mr. Qiu:** Yes, we applied BV ( Bureau VERITAS ) inspection before loading the vessel in China. This is our BV Certificate against the cargo with COs ( certificate of origin ) attached.

**Mr. Masson:** Oh, good. Let's go to the warehouse area to have casual inspection. There are quite a lot of wooden tray and wood packing for your machinery. Do you have phytosanitary certificate accordingly?

**Mr. Qiu:** Yes, all the packing wood has been quarantine fumigation treated in China.

**Mr. Henry:** Here is the Phytosanitary Certificate of the wood packing.

**Mr. Masson:** Open this box please. I need to check the consistency between your cargo and your Packing List.

**Mr. Henry:** The box has been opened. You can check now. You see, these are all the spare parts of the excavators, same as stated in the

Packing List.

**Mr. Qiu:** Our company has been implementing very strict control procedures to get rid of any contraband or other forbidden objects sneaking into our cargo.

**Mr. Masson:** Your team did a good job. Okay, let's go back to the office to calculate your import duty.

**Mr. Henry:** The consignee of the cargo, West-east Highway Project Company has been granted Import Duty Exemption for 6 years as a foreign investment enterprise. You can check its duty exemption certificate.

**Mr. Masson:** Yea, I see. Now, you need to pay the customs clearance fee to the cashier before receiving your Cargo Relieve Certificate.

## Key-words & Expressions

| | |
|---|---|
| Port Authority | 港务局 |
| Shipping Agent | 货运代理 |
| Earth-moving plant | 土方机械 |
| Roller | 压路机 |
| Asphalt paver | 沥青摊铺机 |
| Pile driver | 打桩机 |
| Discharging port | 卸货港 |
| Placing a vessel order | 订船 |
| Total piers length | 码头总长 |
| Terminal for general and bulk cargo | 杂货和散货码头 |
| Berth | 泊位 |
| Bulk cargo vessel | 散货船 |
| Access channel | 通道 |

# CHAPTER III　CONTRACT IMPLEMENTATION OF BOT PROJECT

| | |
|---|---|
| Shore crane | 岸吊 |
| Unloading the vessel | 卸船 |
| Floating crane | 浮吊 |
| Unloading rate | 卸货率 |
| Ship crane | 船吊 |
| Customs Officer | 海关官员 |
| Customs Broker | 报关员 |
| Customs Supervision | 海关监管 |
| Shipment documents | 船运单据 |
| OBL (ocean bill of lading) | 海运提单 |
| Packing List | 装箱单 |
| Commodity inspection | 商检 |
| BV (Bureau VERITAS) inspection | BV (法国国际检验局) 商检 |
| BV Certificate | BV 证书 |
| COs (certificate of origin) | 原产地证书 |
| Casual inspection | 抽检 |
| Phytosanitary certificate | 植物检疫证书 |
| Quarantine fumigation | 检疫熏蒸处理 |
| Spare parts | 备件 |
| Consignee | 收货人 |
| Import Duty Exemption | 免征进口关税 |
| Customs clearance fee | 清关费用 |
| Cargo Relieve Certificate | 货物通关证书 |

# 第14课　从中国进口重型机械

## 对话1

方先生 – 项目公司副总经理

Smith 先生 – 港务局副局长

Hamilton 先生 – 货运代理

**方先生**：我是东西高速公路项目公司的副总经理。这是我的名片。这位是我们的货运代理 Hamilton 先生。由于东西高速公路项目急需进口大量机械和材料，基础设施建设部副部长 Renal 先生建议我来见您。

**Smith 先生**：欢迎，方先生和 Hamilton 先生。Renal 先生昨天已告知我你们要来访。你们打算进口什么机械？

**方先生**：主要是道路和桥梁施工机械，包括大型土方机械、压路机、沥青摊铺机、打桩机、桥梁施工专用机械等。

**Smith 先生**：你们进口机械的总量大约是多少？

**方先生**：噢，太多了。重型施工机械大约需要进口 400 台，加上中小型厂站和设备，总数将超过 1500 台。

**Smith 先生**：数量真大。那我能帮你们什么？

**Hamilton 先生**：您能带我们参观一下你们的港口并介绍一下相关设施吗？我们必须先调查一下卸货港的基本情况再订船。

**Smith 先生**：那是我的荣幸。我们一起到港口转转吧。你们可以看到码头，在海岸沿线的前方。

**方先生**：你们港口的码头总长是多少？

**Smith 先生**：海岸线总长约 1 公里。左边是杂货和散货码头，长度大约 550 米，右边是 400 多米的集装箱码头。

**方先生**：总共有几个泊位？

**Smith 先生**：总共有五个泊位，左边三个，右边两个。根据你们要进口的机械，我想你需要订一艘散货船而不是集装箱船。

**Hamilton 先生**：当然，我们会订散货船。泊位和通道的水深是多少？最大可以进多大的船舶？

**Smith 先生**：杂货和散货泊位水深为 10 米，集装箱泊位水深为 11 米。进港通道的深度超过 13 米。能在本港停泊的船舶最大吨位是 5 万吨。

**Hamilton 先生**：我在这里没见到大型岸吊啊。你们有足够的吊机来卸船吗？

**Smith 先生**：我们只有两台岸吊，一台用于杂货和散货，另一台用于集装箱。但是现在，用于杂货和散货的岸吊正在修理中。我们正在用浮吊来卸货。

Hamilton 先生：在这种情况下，卸货率会受到严重影响。方先生，我想我们需要订一艘自带船吊的船。

Smith 先生：是的，我强烈建议你们订一艘自带船吊的船以确保卸货率。

## 对话 2

裘先生 - 项目公司物资部经理

Masson 先生 - 海关官员

Henry 先生 - 报关员

裘先生：早上好先生。我们是东西高速公路项目公司的。我们所有的货物都已运至海关监管仓库区域。我们可以在这里办理清关手续吗？

Masson 先生：是的，当然。请出示你们的船运单据。

Henry 先生：给您。这是我们的海运提单、装箱单和发票。

Masson 先生：贵方在装货港做过商检吗？

裘先生：是的，我们在中国装船前申请了 BV（法国国际检验局）商检。这是我们货物的 BV 证书和所附 COs（原产地证书）。

Masson 先生：哦，很好。咱们到仓库去做个抽检。你们的机械有很多木制托盘和木制包装。你有相应的植物检疫证书吗？

裘先生：是的，所有的木质包装在中国都做过检疫熏蒸处理。

Henry 先生：这是木质包装的植物检疫证明。

**Masson 先生：** 请打开这个箱子。我需要检查一下你们的货物和装箱单是否一致。

**Henry 先生：** 箱子已经打开了，你现在可以检查了。你看，这些都是挖掘机的备件，和装箱单一致。

**裘先生：** 我们公司一直执行非常严格的管控程序，以防止任何走私或其他违禁物品混入我们的货物中。

**Masson 先生：** 你们的团队做得很好。好的，我们回去办公室计算一下你们的进口税。

**Henry 先生：** 货物的收货人，东西高速公路项目公司作为外商投资企业被免征进口关税 6 年。您可以查一下它的免税证明。

**Masson 先生：** 是的，我明白了。在领取你们的货物通关证书之前，你们需要先在收银台支付清关费用。

# LESSON 15   LOCAL WORKERS RECRUITMENT

## Dialogue 1

**Mr. Fang-Deputy General Manager of Project Company**

**Mr. Jackson-Director of Provincial Labor & Employment Development Department**

**Mrs. Morris-Deputy Director of Provincial Public Health Department**

**Mr. Fang:** Welcome Mr. Jackson and Mrs. Morris. Thank you so much for your kind presence to our office on the first day of our local workers recruitment.

**Mr. Jackson:** This is a big day of your company and of my department either. Thousands of young people in this province have been looking for employment for long time. How could I be absent?

## CHAPTER III  CONTRACT IMPLEMENTATION OF BOT PROJECT

**Mrs. Morris:** Me too. I am very delighted that hundreds of young people will find their jobs here, but in the mean time I am very concerned about the tremendous challenge of infectious disease control.

**Mr. Fang:** Mr. Jackson, I hope you can help us to solve the problem we are facing in local worker's recruitment. Some of the local candidates even don't have their ID card.

**Mr. Jackson:** Oh, this is not a white crow in this country. ID cards have not covered some remote rural areas yet. Don't worry, Mr. Fang, I will call the police chief to send a sergeant here to issue ID cards to them.

**Mr. Fang:** You've done me a great favor. Thank you.

**Mr. Jackson:** Up to now, how many local workers have been recruited?

**Mr. Fang:** Our company is going to recruit 500 local workers this time, and up to now we have received more than 700 applications for employment already. There is a very strict recruitment procedure including several steps, i.e. application, ID authentication, health examination and interview. We can only confirm the acceptance of a local worker until he has positively passed all the steps. Since we will have the Health Examination Reports three days later, I cannot confirm the number of the recruited local workers yet.

**Mr. Jackson:** Three days? It takes quite long time. What kind of health examinations are the local applicants undergoing?

**Mr. Fang:** Except general health check, we requested mainly two sets of health examination items. The first set for ascertaining if the candidate has any disease not suitable to work in the construction site, such as heart trouble, hypertension and physical disability, etc.; and the second set for eliminating any patients with infectious disease including AIDS, cholera, hepatitis, etc. The Health Examination Scheme was made under the advice from Provincial Public Health Department. A lot of thanks to Mrs. Morris.

**Mrs. Morris:** That is my duty and pleasure. Since you are going to mass hundreds of workers in your camp, I hope to inspect the accommodation for the local workers with Mr. Jackson together.

**Mr. Jackson:** Good idea. Mr. Fang, let's go to your camp for the local workers right now.

**Mr. Fang:** Glad to receive your inspection. That couldn't be better. The front is just the camp for local workers. We built it last month.

**Mr. Jackson:** Aha, the houses are all built in containers, aren't they?

**Mr. Fang:** Yes, used 150 containers for this camp, 125 for dormitories, and 25 for canteens, shower rooms, laundries, toilets.

**Mrs. Morris:** Very impressive. You've painted the facade with lovely colors and planted trees in each yard. I'd like to see the fitments inside the rooms.

**Mr. Fang:** This is one typical dormitory transformed from one container. We cut the door and window openings, make the interior wall finishing with thermal insulation, installed wooden floor and equipped air conditioner for the dormitory.

**Mrs. Morris:** There are four beds, one table and one shelf. Why I couldn't find mosquito netting here? This is indeed a high-risk area of malaria.

**Mr. Fang:** We've noticed that and purchased enough mosquito netting sets already. Every local worker will have one set as soon as he has been formally hired.

**Mrs. Morris:** Let's have an inspection to the shower rooms and toilets then.

**Mr. Fang:** We built ten shower rooms with five showers each. You see, there are three solar water heaters above the roof of the shower room. The floor of shower room is of anti-slip ceramic tile, actually, even the canteens and toilets as well.

**Mr. Jackson:** You've built a good camp for local workers. I will come again three days later when you completed your local workers recruitment.

## Dialogue 2

**Mr. Fang-Deputy General Manager of Project Company**

**Mr. Jackson-Director of Provincial Labor & Employment Development Department**

**Mr. Jackson:** Congratulations and appreciations to you, Mr. Fang. Your company has made a successful recruitment, and provided 500 jobs to this province.

**Mr. Fang:** Thank you, Mr. Jackson. You've come at the right time we need you. We are signing Employment Contracts with the local workers according to the model contract specified by your department. There is a special clause regarding social security. Many local workers asked detail questions on this clause, which are beyond the ability of my staffs to answer.

**Mr. Jackson:** It is what I expected. That's why I came here with an official in charge of social security. You'd better organize a meeting for him to explain the social security policy directly to the local workers.

**Mr. Fang:** I assign the human resource manager to organize the meeting immediately, and he will announce the commitment of our company to take the employer's responsibility according to social security policy.

**Mr. Jackson:** Well. Has your company bought insurance for the local workers according to the Labor Law?

**Mr. Fang:** Of course, we have bought Employee's Injury Insurance for all the staffs and workers whether foreign or local.

**Mr. Jackson:** When are you going to send them to the job site?

**Mr. Fang:** The local workers need to receive all-around training before working on site. We arranged one-month training to all local workers, including corporate-culture training and manipulative skill training.

**Mr. Jackson:** You've made a good training schedule. And I suggest you to include disciplinary education in your local workers training.

**Mr. Fang:** Yes, we should have included disciplinary education into our training as an important element. Absolutely, we will follow your instruction in our local workers training. May I invite you to give a speech to all local workers some day?

**Mr. Jackson:** I accept your kind invitation. You'd better contact my assistant to fix the time.

## Key-words & Expressions

| | |
|---|---|
| Recruitment | 招聘 |
| Infectious disease control | 传染病控制 |
| White crow | 稀罕的事物 |
| Hypertension | 高血压 |
| Physical disability | 身体残疾 |
| AIDS | 艾滋病 |
| Cholera | 霍乱 |
| Hepatitis | 肝炎 |
| Facade | 外立面 |
| Thermal insulation | 隔热 |
| Mosquito netting | 蚊帐 |
| Malaria | 疟疾 |
| High-risk area of malaria | 疟疾高发区 |
| Anti-slip ceramic tile | 防滑瓷砖 |
| Solar water heater | 太阳能热水器 |
| Social Security | 社会保险 |
| Employee's Injury Insurance | 雇员工伤保险 |
| Corporate-culture training | 企业文化培训 |
| Manipulative skill training | 操作技能培训 |
| Disciplinary education | 纪律教育 |

# 第15课　招募当地工人

## 对话 1

**方先生** - 项目公司副总经理
**Jackson 先生** - 省劳动就业发展厅厅长
**Morris 夫人** - 省卫生厅副厅长

**方先生**：欢迎 Jackson 先生和 Morris 夫人。非常感谢你们在本地员工招聘的第一天光临我们的办公室。

**Jackson 先生**：今天对贵公司和我们部门来说都是重要的日子。这个省成千上万的年轻人找工作已经找了很长时间啦。我怎么能不来呢？

**Morris 夫人**：我也是。我很高兴数百名年轻人将在这里找到工作，但与此同时，我也非常关注传染病控制的巨大挑战。

**方先生**：Jackson 先生，我希望你能帮助解决我们在当地工人招聘中遇到的问题。一些当地的应聘者甚至连身份证都没有。

**Jackson 先生**：哦，在这个国家这可不是稀罕事儿。身份证还没有覆盖到一些偏远的农村地区。别担心，方先生，我会叫警察局长派一名警官过来给他们签发身份证的。

**方先生**：您帮了我一个大忙啦。谢谢您。

**Jackson 先生**：到目前为止，已经招募了多少本地工人了？

**方先生**：这次我们公司打算招聘 500 名本地工人。到目前为止，我们已经收到了 700 多份求职申请。招聘程序非常严格，包括申请、身份认证、体检和面试几个步骤。我们只有等到该申请人通过所有的步骤才能确认是否录用他。因为我们三天后才会有体检报告，所以这会儿我还不能确定已经录用的当地工人的人数。

**Jackson 先生**：三天？时间好长啊。本地的求职申请者在做什么样的体检啊？

**方先生**：除了一般的体检，我们主要要求做两套体检项目。第一套用于确定应聘者是否患有心脏病、高血压、身体残疾等不适合在建筑工地工作的疾病；第二套用于排除患有艾滋病、霍乱、肝炎等传染病的患者。健康检查方案是根据省卫生厅的建议制定的。非常感谢 Morris 夫人。

**Morris 夫人**：不用谢，这是我的职责所在。因为你们要在营地里聚集数百名工人，我希望和 Jackson 先生一起检查一下本地工人的住宿条件。

**Jackson 先生**：好主意。方先生，我们现在就去你的工人营地吧。

**方先生**：很高兴接受您的检查。那再好不过了。前面就是本地工人的营地，我们上个月才建的。

Jackson 先生：啊哈，这些房子都是用集装箱搭建的，不是吗？

方先生：是的，这个营地共用了 150 个集装箱，其中宿舍用了 125 个，食堂、淋浴室、洗衣房、厕所用了 25 个。

Morris 夫人：真是令人印象深刻啊。你们给外立面刷了可爱的颜色，还在每个院子里种了树。我想看看房间里的设施。

方先生：这是由一个集装箱改造而成的标准宿舍。我们切割出了门窗洞口，用隔热材料对内墙做了装修，并为宿舍安装了木地板和空调。

Morris 夫人：有四张床、一张桌子和一个书架。为什么在这里我找不到蚊帐呢？这里可是真正的疟疾高发区啊。

方先生：我们已经注意到了，并且已经购买了足够的蚊帐。每一个本地工人一旦被正式录用就会有一套的。

Morris 夫人：那我们检查一下淋浴间和厕所吧。

方先生：我们建了 10 个淋浴房，每个淋浴房有 5 个淋浴喷头。你看，淋浴房的屋顶上有三个太阳能热水器。淋浴房的地面是防滑瓷砖，实际上，就连食堂和厕所地都一样。

Jackson 先生：你们为本地工人建了一个很好的营地。三天后当你完成当地工人招聘时，我会再来。

## 对话 2

方先生 - 项目公司副总经理

Jackson 先生 - 省劳动就业发展厅厅长

**Jackson 先生**：祝贺并感谢你，方先生。贵公司既成功完成招聘，又为我省提供了 500 个工作岗位。

**方先生**：谢谢您，Jackson 先生。我们正需要您的时候您就来啦。我们正在按照贵部门规定的合同范本与当地工人签订劳动合同。其中一条是关于社会保险的特别条款。许多本地工人就这一条款提出了细节的问题，我的员工回答不了。

**Jackson 先生**：我预料到了。这就是我和一位负责社会保险的官员一起来的原因。你们最好组织一次会议，让他直接向当地工人解释社保政策吧。

**方先生**：我马上安排人力资源经理组织会议，他会宣布公司按照社保政策承担雇主责任的承诺。

**Jackson 先生**：好，你们公司根据劳动法为当地工人购买保险了吗？

**方先生**：当然，我们为所有的职员和工人都购买了雇员工伤保险，无论是外国人还是本地人。

**Jackson 先生**：你打算什么时候把他们派到工地上去呢？

**方先生**：本地工人到现场工作前须接受全方位的培训。我们为本地工人安排了一个月的培训，包括企业文化培训和操作技能培训。

**Jackson 先生**：你们制定了一个很好的培训计划。我建议你们在本地的工人培训中加入纪律教育。

**方先生**：是的，我们应该把纪律教育作为培训的一个重要内容。我们绝对会遵照您的指示进行本地工人的培训。我可以请您找一天给所有本地工人做一次演讲吗？

**Jackson 先生**：我接受你的盛情邀请。你最好和我的助手联系确定一下时间。

## LESSON 16  PROJECT SECURITY DEPLOYMENTS

### Dialogue 1

**Mr. Fang-Deputy General Manager of Project Company**

**Mr. Webster-Security Advisor**

**Mr. Shao-Security Dept. Manager of Project Company**

**Mr. Fang:** Thank you, Mr. Webster. You've just conducted an instructive training to our staffs in respect of personal security self-protection.

**Mr. Webster:** That's my duty. You are welcome. You did a right thing to organize such training on time, Mr. Fang. Because of the exacerbating public order of this country, people need to receive basic personal security training.

**Mr. Fang:** You are absolutely right. Chinese staffs didn't have any experience and awareness on robbery, kidnapping, terrorist attack. What you have taught them will be very helpful to protect themselves in such dangerous occasions. May we take up more of your time today? I'd like to ask for your advice to our camp security.

**Mr. Webster:** Of course, that shall be my honor to work as your Security Advisor.

**Mr. Fang:** Mr. Shao, our Security Dept. manager, will go around the camp with you to see the security measures we have taken.

**Mr. Shao:** Let's go around, Mr. Webster. I am pleased to hear your advice whenever and wherever.

**Mr. Webster:** I noticed all the enclosure wall of your camp topped with barbed and razor wire. Live wire or dead wire?

**Mr. Shao:** That's live wire connected with 220V power. In case of warning instance, the system will connect the wire with pulsed high-voltage generator automatically and enter 3,000V-6,000V pulse attack working condition.

**Mr. Webster:** I have seen some video cameras around your camp. You have installed video monitoring system already, haven't you?

**Mr. Shao:** Yes, the camp has been equipped with 20 more video cameras for monitoring the whole fencing wall and every corner of the camp yard. We have also four watchtowers along the fencing wall.

**Mr. Webster:** Let me have a look on the top of the watchtower.

**Mr. Shao:** Good idea. On the top of the 6-meter high watchtowers, we can monitor the situation clearly. Look, outside the fencing wall, there is a three-meter wide ditch surrounding our camp.

**Mr. Webster:** You have done a lot for your camp security. However, I still have some suggestions as your supplementary security measures.

**Mr. Shao:** Okay, we can go to Mr. Fang's office so that he can take your suggestions face to face.

**Mr. Fang:** Aha, you have looked around our camp already, Mr. Webster. I am looking for your advice.

**Mr. Webster:** I think I don't need to mention any positive aspects of your camp security. I just like to give you four suggestions. First, I suggest equipping your security team members with walkie-talkie system for instant communication. Then you need to have a powerful alarm system to make everybody aware of state of emergency when the case being. Next, a bulletproof car should be purchased for money drawing/depositing affairs and VIP riding. Finally, I noticed that your guard team almost has no defending strength against the gangsters; you have to hire a security company with armed guards.

**Mr. Fang:** The first three suggestions are constructive and acceptable for our company. We will look for your detail proposal of products recommendation of intercom system, security alarm system and bulletproof car. As for your last suggestion, since the Concession Agreement explicitly stipulates that the government is responsible to assign a military or police troop preventing our camp and jobsite from robbery, kidnapping and terrorist attack, we will not hire armed guards instead.

**Mr. Shao:** We have quite many machines and tools on the jobsite far away from our camp. I found it is very difficult to prevent them from theft on site. Do you have any suggestion in this regard, Mr. Webster?

**Mr. Webster:** I don't suggest keeping your machines and tools on site. In consideration of the thieveries running wild in this country, you have to bring all the valuable machines and tools back to garage adjacent to your camp.

**Mr. Fang:** Good, we will follow your advice. I look for your formal proposal then.

**Mr. Webster:** Okay, I will submit you my formal security proposal early next week.


**Dialogue 2**


**Mr. Fang-Deputy General Manager of Project Company**

**Mr. Simpson-Provincial Police Commander**


**Mr. Fang:** Welcome, Commander Simpson. That is so kind of you to have an inspection to our company and to deploy police for West-east Highway Project security.

**Mr. Simpson:** National Police Commissioner informed me that the President had instructed him to prevent West-east Highway Project from any serious security incidents. Our Provincial Police is incumbent on securing your company and the Project. I came here today to ascertain the security environment of your camp and jobsite, meanwhile debrief your security requirement.

**Mr. Fang:** Thank you. In view of the severe security situation, I would like to ask for two passive security measures from Provincial Police, the one to station a police force adjacent to our camp, and another to implement regular police patrols around the camp and the highway jobsite.

**Mr. Simpson:** No problem. I will order to patrol around your camp and the whole jobsite all day long, especially the nighttime. Allow for day and night shift, I think we need to allocate at least 36 policemen for this station. However, in order to work on that, I need your support.

**Mr. Fang:** What can I do for that?

**Mr. Simpson:** You know Provincial Police has a very tight budget. I don't have money to build a barracks near your camp, and to buy the patrol jeeps neither. Can you build the barracks and provide two jeeps?

**Mr. Fang:** Yes, we can build the barracks for your policemen with necessary furniture, auxiliary facilities. With regard to jeeps, we can provide only for your patrol rather than the ownership. I will assign our drivers driving the jeeps and working with the patrol police.

**Mr. Simpson:** When could my policemen move into new barracks?

**Mr. Fang:** Though we can build the barracks within one month, the delivery of furniture and air conditioners will take two months.

**Mr. Simpson:** In this case, let's start the security patrol for your company two months later.

**Mr. Fang:** No, no, Commander. This is not going to work. I hope Provincial Police to start the patrol in ten days. Our jeeps can pick up the policemen from their original barracks every day.

**Mr. Simpson:** Well, then. I have to leave for Police Headquarters to organize patrol team right now.

**Mr. Fang**: I suggest organizing a joint meeting two days later with the participation of your patrol policemen and our drivers together.

**Mr. Simpson**: Good idea. That's done.

## Key-words & Expressions

| | |
|---|---|
| Personal security self-protection | 个人的安防自我保护 |
| Personal security training | 个人安防培训 |
| Exacerbating public order | 日益恶化的公共秩序 |
| Robbery | 抢劫 |
| Kidnapping | 绑架 |
| Terrorist attack | 恐怖袭击 |
| Barbed and razor wire | 带刺的铁丝网 |
| Live wire/dead wire | 带电铁丝网 / 不带电铁丝网 |
| Pulsed high-voltage generator | 脉冲高压发生器 |
| Video Monitoring System | 视频监控系统 |
| Watchtower | 瞭望塔 |
| Walkie-talkie system | 对讲机系统 |
| Bulletproof car | 防弹车 |
| Intercom system | 对讲机系统 |
| Gangster | 匪徒 |
| Armed guards | 武装警卫人员 |
| Security alarm system | 安保报警系统 |
| Passive security measures | 被动安保措施 |
| Security patrol | 安保巡逻 |
| Barracks | 兵营 |

# 第 16 课　项目安防部署

## 对话 1

**方先生 - 项目公司副总经理**

**Webster 先生 - 安保顾问**

**邵先生 - 项目公司安保部门经理**

**方先生：**Webster 先生，谢谢您刚才为我们的员工作了个人安防自我保护方面的指导性培训。

**Webster 先生：**这是我的职责，你不用谢我。方先生，您及时组织这样的培训很对。由于这个国家公共秩序的日益恶化，人们需要接受基本的个人安防培训。

**方先生：**您说得完全正确。中国员工对抢劫、绑架、恐怖袭击没有任何经验和意识。您教给他们的东西对他们在这样危险的场合保护自己会很有帮助。我们今天可以占用您更多的时间吗？

我想征求您对我们营地安保的建议。

**Webster 先生：** 当然，我很荣幸能成为你们的安保顾问。

**方先生：** 我们的安保部经理邵先生将陪您一起到营地看看我们采取的安保措施。

**邵先生：** 我们走吧，Webster 先生。那么我就洗耳恭听您随时随地给我建议咯。

**Webster 先生：** 我注意到你们营地的围墙上都装有带刺的铁丝网。是通电的还是不通电的？

**邵先生：** 那是通了 220V 电的带电铁丝网。一旦报警，系统将自动把线路与脉冲高压发生器连接，进入 3000V–6000V 脉冲攻击工况。

**Webster 先生：** 我在你们的营地周围看到了一些摄像机。你们已经安装了视频监控系统，是吗？

**邵先生：** 是的，营地配备了 20 多台摄像机，监控整个围墙和营地院子的每个角落。沿着围墙我们还有四个瞭望塔。

**Webster 先生：** 让我去瞭望塔的顶部看看。

**邵先生：** 好主意。在 6 米高的瞭望塔上，我们可以清楚地监察形势。你看，在围墙外面还有一条 3 米宽的沟渠围绕着我们的营地。

**Webster 先生：** 你们为营地安全做了很多啊。不过我还是有一些建议作为你们的补充安全措施。

**邵先生：** 好的，我们可以去方先生的办公室，让他能当面听取您的建议。

**方先生：** 啊哈，Webster 先生，您已经看过我们的营地啦。我期待您的建议。

**Webster 先生：**我想我没必要来谈你们营地安防做得好的方面了。我只想给你们四个建议。首先，我建议给你们的安保小组成员配备对讲机系统，以便即时沟通。第二，你们需要一个强大的报警系统，当紧急情况发生时让所有人都能知道。三是购置防弹车，用于办理取款／存款业务和贵宾搭乘。最后，我注意到你们的警卫队几乎没有抵御匪徒的防卫力量，你们必须雇用一个有武装警卫的保安公司。

**方先生：**前三个建议是建设性的，我们公司都可以接受。我们还盼着您关于对讲系统、安防报警系统和防弹车产品推荐的详细提议呢。关于您的最后一个建议，由于特许经营权协议明确规定政府有责任派遣军队或警察部队，保护我们的营地和工地免遭抢劫、绑架和恐怖袭击，因此我们不会雇佣武装警卫。

**邵先生：**我们在远离营地的工地上有很多机械和工具。我发现在现场很难防止它们被盗。在这方面您有什么建议吗，Webster 先生？

**Webster 先生：**我建议你们不要把机械和工具留在现场。考虑到这个国家的盗贼猖獗，你们必须把所有贵重的机械和工具运回营地附近的车库里。

**方先生：**好的，我们会听从您的建议。我期待您的正式建议书。

**Webster 先生：**好的，我将在下周初向您提交我的正式安保建议书。

### 对话 2

**方先生 - 项目公司副总经理**

**Simpson 先生 - 省警署署长**

**方先生**：欢迎，Simpson 署长。您能来我公司视察，并为东西高速公路工程安全部署警力，真是太好了。

**Simpson 先生**：国家警察总署署长告诉我，总统已经指示他防止东西高速公路项目发生任何严重的安防事件。我省警方有责任保护贵公司和项目的安全。我今天来是想了解一下你们营地和工地的安全环境，同时听取你们的安防要求。

**方先生**：谢谢您。鉴于严峻的安防形势，我想请省警方采取两项被动安全措施，一项是在营地附近部署驻扎一支警队，另一项是在营地和公路工地周围实施定期警察巡逻。

**Simpson 先生**：没问题。我会下令在你们的营地和整个工地全天候巡逻，尤其是晚上。考虑到白班和夜班，我想我们至少需要为这个警站配备 36 名警察。但是要那么做，我需要你们的支持。

**方先生**：我能为此做些什么？

**Simpson 先生**：你知道省警署的预算很紧张。我们没有钱在你们营地附近建营房，也没有钱买巡逻吉普车。你们能建造营房并提供两辆吉普车吗？

**方先生**：是的，我们可以为警察建造营房，并配备必要的家具和辅助设施。关于吉普车，我们只能提供给你巡逻，不能给予所有权。我会指派我们的司机驾驶吉普车，并与巡逻警察合作。

**Simpson 先生**：我的警察什么时候能搬进新营房呢？

**方先生**：虽然我们可以在一个月内建好营房，但是家具和空调需要两个月的时间才能运到。

**Simpson 先生**：这样的话，让我们两个月后开始为你公司的安全巡逻吧。

**方先生：** 不，不，长官。这可不行啊！我希望省警署十天内开始巡逻。我们的吉普车可以每天到原来的营房里去接警察的。

**Simpson 先生：** 那好吧。我必须走了，得回警署去组织巡逻队。

**方先生：** 我建议两天后组织一次联席会议，由你们的巡逻警察和我们的司机共同参加。

**Simpson 先生：** 好主意。一言为定。

## LESSON 17  FULFILLING SOCIAL RESPONSIBILITIES

### Dialogue

Mr. Mason-Principal of Friendship Vocational School

Mr. Bird-Village Head

Mr. Morgan-Student Representative of Friendship Vocational School

Mr. Liang-General Manager of Project Company

Mr. Gao-Ambassador of China

Mr. Godwin-Provincial Governor

**Mr. Mason:** Good morning, ladies and gentlemen. I am the principal of the newly established Friendship Vocational School. Thank you for your kind presence to inauguration ceremony of our school.

Especially thanks to honorable provincial governor Mr. Godwin, Honorable ambassador of China Mr. Gao and general manager of West-east Highway Project Company Mr. Liang for their full support in Friendship Vocational School's funding and setting up. Now, let's give enthusiastic applause to welcome them unveiling nameplate of our school.

**Mr. Mason:** Now, let's welcome the local village head Mr. Bird to have a speech.

**Mr. Bird:** Congratulations to all students and faculty of Friendship Vocational School. The opening of your school is one more joyful event in this antiquated land since the commencement of construction of West-east Highway one year ago. Presenting all my villagers, I would like hereby to express deep gratitude to West-east Highway Project Company who brings so many wonderful changes to our life. These Chinese workers have paved motor road connecting our village to the highway, dug wells providing tap water, offered mobile medical service, built primary school etc. All our villagers appreciate your free and kind help. You are not only a Chinese contractor, you are our brothers. Thank you again, our Chinese brothers.

**Mr. Mason:** Thanks to Mr. Bird for his genuine and emotional speech. Now our Student Representative Mr. Morgan is going to give his words.

**Mr. Morgan:** I am very excited to be a student of Friendship Vocational School after being deprived of education for three years. Technology is developing rapidly; the World is changing rapidly. We have to learn how to catch up the paces of development. All my schoolfellows are eager for learning knowledge, skill in order to be people of value like these Chinese workers. I hereby express the resolution of all my schoolfellows, observing discipline, respecting teachers, learning hard and being ready to contribute to the development of our hometown and our country.

**Mr. Mason:** Mr. Morgan made his great resolution. The teachers of our school and I will definitely help the students in realizing their ideality. Let's welcome the sponsor of our school, general manager of West-east Highway Project Company Mr. Liang to give us his speech.

**Mr. Liang:** Today I am extremely happy, because Friendship Vocational School is finally opened after getting over so many difficulties and barriers. We are grateful to your country's trust and awarding West-east Highway Project to our company. As an old Chinese saying goes that one should pay back when he receives favor. We have been paying back to this country and society by helping the villagers and donating this School. Village head Mr. Bird calls us Chinese brothers. It makes me feel that all we have done for the villagers are worthy. Student Morgan's speech makes me feel more responsibility to the young generation of this country. Our company is a contractor and I am a business man. In my opinion, money and treasure are not the full objectives of business. Helping the people and building a better world give full meaning to our business. President of China Xi Jinping instructed Chinese contractors working abroad "to dedicate before request, and dedicate more than request". West-east Highway Project Company will always follow President Xi Jinping's instruction and fulfill our social responsibilities along with the construction and operation of West-east Highway.

**Mr. Mason:** Thanks to Mr. Liang for his impressive speech. Let's welcome China's ambassador Mr. Gao having a speech.

**Mr. Gao:** I would like hereby to extend my warm congratulations upon the inauguration of Friendship Vocational School on behalf of China's Embassy. West-east Highway Project Company has done the right things benefit to the villagers along the highway and society of this country. The government of China requests all the Chinese enterprises fulfilling social responsibilities in their overseas business, strictly observing host country's laws and regulations, substantially protecting local environment, attentively creating local jobs, sincerely helping local communities. I hope and believe all the other Chinese companies working in this country will take West-east Highway Project Company as an example to lift their performance in fulfilling social responsibilities.

**Mr. Mason:** Thank you, ambassador. We really appreciate what Chinese companies have contributed for this country. Let us applause to the last speaker Mr. Godwin, the provincial governor.

**Mr. Godwin:** Today is a big day of our province, because inauguration of Friendship Vocational School is a great event of our province. By this event, young people in the province will find opportunities to receive vocational education and training, therewith grow into the talents for provincial reconstruction. By this event, we will find more opportunities to learn knowledge, skills and experiences from our Chinese brothers in economic and social development. Students of Friendship Vocational School, I request you to seize your opportunity, learning hard in this school, getting ready to reconstruct your hometown with extensive expertise, proficient skill and dedicated attitude. Faculty of Friendship Vocational School, I request you cooperate with Chinese colleagues sincerely and closely, building this school into the best one of our province. Ambassador

Mr. Gao and general manager Mr. Liang, I appreciate your kind and constant support, and would like to make early appointments with you for joint inspection to this school every quarter, monitoring the performance of the school and solving any major problem in the school operation. Do you agree?

**Mr. Gao:** I fully agree with you, honorable governor.

**Mr. Liang:** That's a wonderful idea. I agree as well, honorable governor.

**Mr. Mason:** I hereby represent the faculty team of Friendship Vocational School making a commitment to try our best in solidarity, conscientiousness, strictness and innovation. We will educate and train our students according to the demand and requirement of provincial reconstruction, and be ready to receive your inspection and listen to your instruction every quarter.

Now, the Inauguration Ceremony of Friendship Vocational School ends here.

## Key-words & Expressions

| | |
|---|---|
| Social responsibilities | 社会责任 |
| Inauguration ceremony | 落成仪式，开学典礼 |
| Vocational school | 职业学校 |
| Enthusiastic applause | 热情鼓掌 |
| Unveiling nameplate | 揭牌 |
| Faculty | 教职工 |
| Motor road | 汽车路，机动车路 |
| Mobile medical service | 流动医疗服务 |
| Be deprived of education | 失学 |

| | |
|---|---|
| Sponsor | 赞助人 |
| Pay back when one receives favor | 知恩图报 |
| To dedicate before request, and dedicate more than request | 先予后取,多予少取 |
| Extensive expertise | 渊博的专业知识 |
| Proficient skill | 娴熟的技能 |
| Dedicated attitude | 敬业的态度 |
| Solidarity | 团结 |
| Conscientiousness | 尽职 |
| Strictness | 严谨 |
| Innovation | 创新 |

# 第 17 课　履行社会责任

## 对话

Mason 先生 - 友谊职业学校校长

Bird 先生 - 村长

Morgan 先生 - 友谊职业学校学生代表

梁先生 - 项目公司总经理

高先生 - 中国大使

Godwin 先生 - 省长

**Mason 先生：** 早上好，女士们、先生们。我是新成立的友谊职业学校的校长。感谢你们出席我校的落成仪式。特别要感谢尊敬的省长 Godwin 先生、尊敬的中国大使高先生和东西高速公路项目公司总经理梁先生对友谊职业学校的资助和创办给予的全力支持。现在，让我们以热烈的掌声欢迎他们为我们学校揭牌。

**Mason 先生**：现在让我们欢迎本地村长 Bird 先生发言。

**Bird 先生**：祝贺友谊职业学校全体师生员工。你们学校的开学，是自一年前东西高速公路开工建设以来，这片古老土地上又一件喜事。在此，我代表我的乡亲们，向东西高速公路项目公司表示深深的谢意，是你们给我们的生活带来了如此多美好的改变。这些中国工人铺设了连接我们村庄和高速公路的机动车路、挖了提供自来水的水井、提供了流动医疗服务、修建了小学等等。我们全体村民都感谢你们的慷慨帮助。你们不仅是中国的承包商，更是我们的兄弟。再次感谢我们的中国兄弟。

**Mason 先生**：感谢 Bird 先生真心实意的演讲。现在由我们的学生代表 Morgan 先生发言。

**Morgan 先生**：在失学了三年之后，我非常高兴能成为友谊职业学校的一名学生。技术在迅速发展，世界在迅速变化。我们必须学会跟上发展的步伐。我所有的同学都渴望学习知识和技能，以便成为像这些中国工人一样有价值的人。我谨在此表达全体同学的决心，遵守纪律、尊师重教、努力学习，准备好为家乡和祖国的发展贡献自己的力量。

**Mason 先生**：摩根先生下了很大的决心。我和我们学校的老师一定会帮助学生实现他们的理想。下面有请我校赞助商——东西高速公路项目公司总经理梁先生致辞。

**梁先生**：今天我非常高兴，因为友谊职业学校在克服了这么多困难和障碍后终于开学了。感谢贵国对我公司的信任，并将东西高速公路项目授予我公司。中国有句古话叫"知恩图报"。通过帮助村民和捐赠这所学校，我们一直在回报这个国家和社会。村长 Bird 先生称我们是中国兄弟。这让我觉得我们为村民所做的一切都是值得的。Morgan 同学的演讲让我觉得自己对这个国家的年轻一代负有更多的责任。我们公司是承包商，我是个商人。

在我看来，金钱和财富并不是商业的全部目标。帮助人民和建设一个更美好的世界，让我们生意有了完整的意义。中国国家主席习近平指示在海外工作的中国承包商"先予后取，多予少取"。东西高速公路项目公司将一如既往地遵从习近平主席的指示，在东西高速公路建设和运营当中履行我们的社会责任。

**Mason 先生**：感谢梁先生的精彩演讲。让我们欢迎中国大使黄先生讲话。

**黄先生**：我谨代表中国大使馆对友谊职业学校的成立表示热烈祝贺。东西高速公路项目公司做了正确的事情，造福了公路沿线的村民和社会。中国政府要求所有中国企业在海外经营中履行社会责任、严格遵守所在国法律法规、切实保护当地环境、用心创造当地就业机会、真诚帮助当地社区。我希望并相信所有在这个国家工作的中国公司都能以东西高速公路项目公司为榜样，提升其履行社会责任的表现。

**Mason 先生**：谢谢您，大使。我们真心感谢中国公司为这个国家所做的贡献。让我们给最后一位发言者省长 Godwin 先生献上热烈的掌声。

**Godwin 先生**：今天是我省的一个大日子，因为友谊职业学校的落成仪式是我省的一件大事。通过这次活动，我省青年将有机会接受职业教育和培训，从而成长为我省重建的人才。通过这次活动，我们将有更多机会向中国兄弟学习经济和社会发展方面的知识、技能和经验。友谊职业学校的同学们，请你们抓住机遇，在这所学校努力学习，以渊博的专业知识、娴熟的技能和敬业的态度，为重建家乡做好准备。友谊职业学校的全体老师们，请你们与中国同事真诚而紧密的合作，把这所学校建设成为我省最好的学校。黄大使、梁总经理，感谢你们一直以来的鼎力支持，我愿意与你们提前预约，每季度到本校进行联合检查，监督学校运行情况，解决学校运行中的重大问题。你们同意吗？

**黄先生：** 我完全同意，尊敬的省长。

**梁先生：** 真是个好主意。我也同意，尊敬的省长。

**Mason 先生：** 我谨代表友谊职业学校的教师队伍郑重承诺，尽最大努力做到团结、尽职、严谨、创新。我们将按本省重建的需求和要求来教育和培训学生，每季度接受你们的检查和指导。

友谊职业学校落成典礼到此结束。

## LESSON 18  WHOLE ROAD OPENING TO TRAFFIC

### Dialogue

**Mr. Liang**-General Manager of Project Company

**Mr. Fang**-Deputy General Manager of Project Company

**Mr. Peng**-Chief Engineer of Project Company

**Mrs. Diana**-Highway Tolling Department Manager of Project Company

**Mr. Sheriff**-Highway Administration Department Manager of Project Company

**Mr. Rock**-Highway Maintenance Department Manager of Project Company

**Mr. Liang:** Two months ago, we launched a campaign named 100-

day to Grand Opening. We have made great achievement within the last two months in both construction progress and road administration preparation. Three new departments, i.e. Highway Tolling Department, Highway Administration Department and Highway Maintenance Department have been established. But there are still quite a lot of activities behind the schedule. Although I know everyone is very busy right now, we have to have a meeting this evening to review our progress and identify all the critical works to the Grand Opening of West-east Highway. Please briefly report the relevant aspects within your responsibility. Mr. Peng first please.

**Mr. Peng:** By the end of last month, the 600 km pavement of West-east Highway has been entirely completed. To the Grand Opening, we still remain some critical works as below. The first, slight water seepage was found in two tunnels along the highway; the second, 6 percent of total 1,685 linear km side barrier and median barrier remain to be installed; the third, 22 percent of road line remains to be marked; the fourth, road signage posts have been wholly settled, but 4 percent of the signage plates have not been delivered to site yet from China; the last, all the toll booths have been built with 92 percent mechanical stop levers in place, that means remaining 8 percent of mechanical stop levers should be installed.

**Mr. Liang:** What are your measures to these issues?

**Mr. Peng:** The tunnel subcontractor has organized a special team of high-pressure grouting and submitted a repairing scheme. I just hosted an experts' meeting this morning to perfect and approve the scheme. The tunnel subcontractor will bring it into implementation immediately. The water seepage at the tunnel walls can be blocked within a week. Regarding the barriers, road lines and mechanical stop

## CHAPTER III  CONTRACT IMPLEMENTATION OF BOT PROJECT

levers, we are organizing double work teams to accelerate the progress and ensure the completion of the works within two weeks. The real problem is the undelivered signage plates, we are not able to complete the signage works without the plates.

**Mr. Liang:** I have noted down the problem of signage plates. Then, the next please, Mrs. Diana.

**Mrs. Diana:** Half year ago, our company sent 24 local staffs to China for highway tolling system visit and training. I am so grateful to our company for being one of the above staffs trained. As soon as we come back from China, five toll collector training courses were conducted and around 300 local staffs received training. We have allocated each toll collector to a certain toll station and made furniture ready in all the toll booths. Up to now, the only problem is the absence of barcode printers and scanners. We hope the barcode printers and scanners will be delivered to site at least half month before the whole road opening, so that our toll collectors will have enough time to practice and get familiar with the barcode system.

**Mr. Liang:** Okay, I got your point. Mr. Sheriff please.

**Mr. Sheriff:** I'd like to report that our proposed West-east Highway Administration Regulation and Standard Toll List were finally approved by National Highway Administration Authority 10 days ago. The Posters for Highway Administration Regulation, Standard Toll and Driving Safety Reminders have been designed and could be turned over to the printing shop after review and approval by company management. Our department is focusing on the preparation of West-east Highway Website recently.

**Mr. Liang:** Please tell me the preparation progress of highway service areas.

**Mr. Sheriff:** The gas stations in our five proposed service areas are ready for operation. One beverage vending machine has been allocated in each service area. But the shops in the service areas will not be ready before the Grand Opening.

**Mr. Liang:** What about the wrecker service arrangement?

**Mr. Sheriff:** We are negotiating with three potential wrecker service companies. We are going to select two of them and sign service contract next week.

**Mr. Liang:** Please submit your draft of service contract to Mr. Fang for review and approval before signing. Mr. Rock please, it's your turn now.

**Mr. Rock:** Our department has held meetings with the work teams of each section of the highway and signed Letter of Assurance for the emergency repair and regular maintenance during the Defects Notification Period. An Emergency Report & Response Mechanism has been established against sudden damage of any section of the highway. Our department is going to make an inspection tour to all the emergency crews in the coming month before the Grand Opening.

**Mr. Liang:** Good, well prepared. Mr. Fang, what is your solution to the undelivered goods urgently needed for the Whole Line Opening?

**Mr. Fang:** I think we have no choice other than air transport right now. I will instruct the Logistic Department to consign barcode printers, scanners and traffic signage plates by air freight next week.

**Mr. Liang:** Okay, Mr. Fang, you have to make the necessary goods on site within 10 days. Can you promise?

**Mr. Fang:** Sure, I commit that.

**Mr. Liang:** According to the reports and arrangements on this meeting, I believe we will have all the conditions ready for Whole Line Opening within 20 days. I will invite the minister of Infrastructure Development and the director of National Highway Administration Authority to make an inspection on West-east Highway 25 days later, and ask them to sign consent to the commercial operation of this highway. I hereby request all the departments and all the staffs of the company make every endeavor to the destination of Grand Opening from now on, and turn the commercial operation of whole line into a reality. Finally, I'd like to ask Mr. Fang presenting the agenda of Whole Line Opening Ceremony.

**Mr. Fang:** We scheduled the Whole Line Opening Ceremony on the second Friday next month; it means exact 40 days later. Several ministers, China's ambassador and quite many VIPs will attend. The minister of Infrastructure Development, the director of National Highway Administration Authority, the governor of the province, the ambassador of China and the president of our mother corporation will make their speech and cut the ribbon on the ceremony. A three-minute video about the construction of the highway will be presented, and 20 most valuable contributors will be awarded. At the end of the ceremony, the government officials and VIPs will grant Toll Free Coupons to the first 500 vehicle-drivers on road.

**Mr. Liang:** Sounds very exciting. Mr. Fang, you shall be in charge of invitation, venue preparation and ribbon-cut etc. Then three-minute video preparation and 20 MVCs' recommendation shall be in charged by Mr. Peng. And Mrs. Diana, print 500 Toll Free Coupons in advance please. So much for today's meeting.

## Key-words & Expressions

| | |
|---|---|
| Grand Opening | 通车典礼 |
| Highway Tolling Department | 高速公路收费部 |
| Highway Administration Department | 高速公路路政部 |
| Highway Maintenance Department | 高速公路养护部 |
| Water seepage | 渗水 |
| Side barrier/median barrier | 路侧护栏/中央护栏 |
| Road signage post | 道路标识杆 |
| Signage plate | 标识牌 |
| Toll booth | 收费亭 |
| Mechanical stop lever | 机械挡车杆 |
| High-pressure grouting | 高压注浆 |
| Repairing Scheme | 修复方案 |
| Toll collector | 收费员 |
| Barcode printer | 条形码打印机 |
| Scanner | 扫码器 |
| Standard Toll List | 过路费标准费率表 |
| Beverage vending machine | 饮料自动售卖机 |
| Wrecker service | 拖车清障服务 |
| Letter of Assurance | 保证书 |
| Defects Notification Period | 缺陷通知期 |
| Emergency Report & Response Mechanism | 应急报告和响应机制 |
| Air freight | 空运 |
| Whole Line Opening Ceremony | 全线通车仪式 |
| MVC ( Most Valuable Contributor ) | 最有价值贡献者 |
| Toll Free Coupon | 免过路费优惠券 |
| Ribbon-cut | 剪彩 |

## 第18课　全线通车

对话

梁先生 - 项目公司总经理

方先生 - 项目公司副总经理

彭先生 - 项目公司总工程师

Diana 夫人 - 项目公司高速公路收费部经理

Sheriff 先生 - 项目公司高速公路路政部经理

Rock 先生 - 项目公司高速公路养护部经理

**梁先生**：两个月前，我们发起了一个名为"奋战100天，保通车典礼"的活动。近两个月来，我们在施工进度和公路管理准备方面都取得了很好的成绩。新组建了高速公路收费部、高速公路路政部、高速公路养护部三个部门。但是我们仍然有很多事项落后于预定计划。虽然我知道大家现在都非常忙，但今晚我们不得不召开这个会议,检查我们的进度,确定保障东西高速公路通车典礼的各项关键工作。请各位简要汇报一下你们所负责的相关方面。请彭先生先来。

**彭先生**:截至上月底,东西高速公路600公里的路面铺设工作已全部完成。对于通车典礼,我们仍有以下重要的工作要做。一是公路沿线两条隧道有轻微渗水现象;二是总共1685延千米的路侧护栏和中央护栏还有6%需要安装;三是22%的道路标线需要标划;四是道路标识杆已经全部安装好,但是4%的标识牌还未从中国运到现场;最后,所有收费亭和92%的机械停挡车杆都已安装完毕,这意味着还剩8%的机械挡车杆须安装到位。

**梁先生**:对这些问题你们采取什么措施啊?

**彭先生**:隧道分包商已经组织了高压灌浆专项小组并提交了修复方案。就在今天上午我主持召开了一次专家会议,完善并通过了这个方案。隧道分包商将立即付诸实施。隧道墙体的渗水可以在一周内被堵住。关于护栏、道路标线和机械挡车杆,我们正在组织两组人员来加快进度,以确保在两周内完成工作。真正成问题的是标识牌还未到场,没有标识牌我们无法完成道路标识的工作啊。

**梁先生**:标识牌的问题我已经记下了。那么下一位,Diana夫人。

**Diana夫人**:半年前,我公司派出24名当地员工赴中国进行高速公路收费系统的考察和培训。对自己也成为我们公司上述培训人员中的一员,我非常感激。从中国回来后,我们就举办了5期收费员培训班,约300名当地工作人员接受了培训。每个收费员都已经被指派到特定的收费站,而且所有收费亭中的家具都已准备好。到目前为止,我们唯一的问题是没有条形码打印机和扫描器。我们希望条码打印机和扫描器最晚在整条道路开通前半个月送到现场,这样我们的收费员就有足够的时间练习和熟悉条码系统。

**梁先生**:好的,我明白你的意思了。Sheriff 先生请。

**Sheriff 先生**:我想报告一下,我们提交的《东西公路管理条例》和《过路费费率表》终于在 10 天前得到了国家公路管理局的批准。《公路管理条例》、《过路费费率》、《行车安全提示》的海报已经设计完成,经公司管理层审核批准后,就可以交印刷店付印。我们部门最近正集中精力准备东西高速公路网站。

**梁先生**:请告诉我高速公路服务区的准备情况。

**Sheriff 先生**:我们五个拟建服务区内的加油站已准备投入运营。每个服务区都配备了一台饮料自动售卖机。但是服务区的商店在通车典礼之前还准备不好。

**梁先生**:那么拖车清障服务的安排呢?

**Sheriff 先生**:我们正在与三家潜在的拖车清障服务公司谈判。我们将在下周选择其中的两家并签订服务合同。

**梁先生**:请将拖车清障服务合同草稿提交给方先生审核后再签字。Rock 先生,现在轮到你了。

**Rock 先生**:我部已与高速公路各路段施工团队召开了会议,并签署了缺陷通知期内进行紧急维修和定期维护的保证书。针对高速公路任何路段的突发性损坏,建立了应急报告和响应机制。下个月,我们部门将在通车典礼前对所有抢修队进行一次巡视。

**梁先生**:很好,准备得很充分。方先生,对于全线通车所急需的未交付货物,你有什么解决方案?

**方先生**:除了空运,我想我们现在别无选择。我会指示物资部在下周就空运条码打印机、扫描器和交通标识牌。

**梁先生：** 好的，方先生，你必须在 10 天内把必要的货物运到现场。你能保证吗？

**方先生：** 当然，我保证。

**梁先生：** 根据这次会议的汇报和安排，我相信 20 天内我们将具备全线通车的所有条件。25 天后，我将邀请基础设施建设部部长和国家公路管理局局长对东西高速公路进行检查，并请他们签署同意该高速公路投入商业运营。我在此要求公司各部门和全体员工，从现在起，向通车典礼的目标全力冲刺，把全线商业运营变成现实。最后，我想请方先生介绍全线通车仪式的议程安排。

**方先生：** 我们计划在下个月的第二个星期五举行全线通车仪式，也就是 40 天后。几位部长、中国大使和许多重要人物将会出席。基础设施建设部部长、国家公路管理局局长、省长、中国大使和我们母公司的总裁将在仪式上致辞并剪彩。将播放一段关于高速公路建设的 3 分钟视频，并奖励 20 位最有价值的贡献者。仪式的最后，政府官员和贵宾们将向首批上路的 500 名司机发放免费优惠券。

**梁先生：** 听起来很令人兴奋。方先生，您来负责邀请函、场地筹备、剪彩等工作。那么 3 分钟的视频准备和 20 位最有价值贡献者的推荐就由彭先生负责。还有，请 Diana 夫人提前印制 500 张免费优惠券。今天的会议到此结束。

## LESSON 19  HIGHWAY OPERATION & MAINTENANCE

### Dialogue 1

**Mr. Fang**-Deputy General Manager of Project Company

**Mr. Douglas**-Deputy Director of National Highway Administration Authority

**Mr. Rock**-Highway Maintenance Department Manager of Project Company

**Mr. Sheriff**-Highway Administration Department Manager of Project Company

**Mr. Douglas:** Good morning Mr. Fang. Do you welcome me as an uninvited visitor today?

**Mr. Fang:** Oh, welcome, Mr. Douglas. We always welcome your distinguished guest. What can I do for you?

**Mr. Douglas:** I received an Annual Operation Report on West-east Highway from your company ten days ago. The report says the highway is under regular maintenance and traffic safety has been well secured. For verification, I would like to have an on-the-spot inspection today.

**Mr. Fang:** That's our pleasure to receive your kind inspection any time. What are you going to inspect today and where would you like to start your inspection?

**Mr. Douglas:** I want to see the real situation of highway maintenance and operation directly instead of reading a report. First of all, please show me the machinery of your highway maintenance team.

**Mr. Fang:** I see. Please allow me to introduce our Highway Maintenance Department manager Mr. Rock and Highway Administration Department manager Mr. Sheriff.

**Mr. Douglas:** Nice to meet you, Mr. Rock and Mr. Sheriff.

**Mr. Rock:** Me too, Mr. Douglas. That's my honor to show you one of our four machinery stations supporting the West-east Highway maintenance. You see, there are two breakers, six backhoe excavators, eight loaders, fifteen dump trucks, one multi-function asphalt paver, four vibro-rollers and one set of asphalt concrete mix station.

**Mr. Douglas:** I believe most of these machines were used during the highway construction period. Are these machines still keeping with a stable availability rate nowadays?

**Mr. Rock:** Yes, we have been keeping an average machinery availability rate over 90%. We set up a well-equipped overhaul shop in each machinery station and all the machines are under regular and elaborate maintenance.

**Mr. Douglas:** That sounds good. What is the brand-new machine over there?

**Mr. Rock:** That is a new Caterpillar pavement milling machine just purchased from US. You may be aware, too many heavy vehicles on the highway were much overloaded and made deep tracks on the road surface. By this pavement milling machine, we can eliminate the unevenness and improve the road surface of certain section in the midnight, and ensure opening a smooth traffic next early morning.

**Mr. Douglas:** Nice machine. Maintaining safe and smooth traffic on the highways has always been the primary goal of our administration. Mr. Fang, let me see your substantial measures achieving this target.

**Mr. Fang:** Mr. Sheriff, this is your turn now.

**Mr. Sheriff:** Sure. We'd better get on a jeep and see the traffic safety measures along the highway.

**Mr. Douglas:** Good idea. Let's go.

**Mr. Fang:** In order to get rid of the traffic disturbance from the entry of human and livestock, our company has built enclosures by the side of highway in certain sensitive sections.

**Mr. Douglas:** I have seen the fence along the highway. It safeguards the smooth flow of automobile effectively.

**Mr. Sheriff:** Our company has upgraded the traffic signage system of the highway. The new signage is more conspicuous and systematic reminding the vehicle's drivers to keep the right way of driving.

**Mr. Douglas:** What are your measures against the night driving accidents?

**Mr. Sheriff:** We have taken two measures. Firstly, reflective paint has been applied at the curves of highway; and secondly, anti-glare panels have been installed above the median barrier.

**Mr. Douglas:** How about the effect of your measures?

**Mr. Sheriff:** Quite satisfactory. The fatal accidents have been greatly reduced. Last year, the fatality rate per 100 million vehicle-km descended to 6 from 8 of the year before last year.

**Mr. Douglas:** You did a good job in highway safety management.

**Mr. Fang:** But I think the current traffic accident rate is still at a high level including fatal crashes, injury crashes and PDO (property damage only) crashes. Alcohol-related accidents kept as the majority in the statistic. We really need your support in drunk-driving control.

**Mr. Douglas:** Absolutely, National Highway Administration Authority will do its best in this regard.


### Dialogue 2

**Mrs. Diana-Highway Tolling Department Manager of Project Company**

**Mr. Roland-Toll Regulator of National Highway Administration Authority**

**Mrs. Diana:** Good afternoon, Mr. Roland. I'm sorry to bother you again today.

**Mr. Roland:** Oh, Mrs. Diana. What's wrong about your highway toll income? Are you going to apply for government compensation on account of low traffic flow again?

**Mrs. Diana:** No, I am not coming for the government compensation today. The vehicle flow rate of our highway is persistently increasing recently. But you see, the price of commodities is rising rapidly, while our highway toll rate has been kept at a low level for a long time. I noticed that the increase in CPI over the last 6 months exceeds fifteen percent. In account of all the operation cost including reimbursement of bank loan, it's even impossible to maintain a positive cash flow under such a low toll rate level. Do you think our company has the reason to apply for an increase of the toll levels?

**Mr. Roland:** Yes, you are right. By virtue of the Toll Road Act, when the increase in CPI over the most recent six months exceeds twenty five percent per annum, the highway developer may apply for toll level increase subject to two conditions. The one, the increase in CPI in the period since the most recent toll increase has been greater than 5%; and another, the toll levels applied should not be higher than the Capped Toll Level for that period.

**Mrs. Diana:** No problem. Actually, our toll levels have never been raised since the very beginning of highway commercial operation. We will certainly apply the toll levels increase in accordance with the Capped Toll Level. May you explain what the current Capped Toll Level is?

**Mr. Roland:** The Capped Toll Level is calculated based on the formulae outlined in the Tolling Policy. Let's find a day we're both free, I will show you the formulae and tell you how to calculate the Capped Toll Level.

**Mrs. Diana:** Thank you, Mr. Roland. May I have an application form for the toll levels increase?

**Mr. Roland:** Of course, here you are. You can take it back and fill in it. As long as the toll levels you applied are at or below the Capped Toll Level, I will approve them in accordance with the terms of the Tolling Policy and all relevant laws.

**Mrs. Diana:** How long will our company receive your granting permission after submission of the application?

**Mr. Roland:** It depends, because I must obtain the written approval of the minister of transportation prior to granting permission.

## Key-words & Expressions

| | |
|---|---|
| On-the-spot inspection | 现场检查 |
| Availability rate | 可用率，完好率 |
| Overhaul shop | 检修车间 |
| Caterpillar | 卡特彼勒（美国重型工程机械制造商） |
| Pavement milling machine | 路面铣刨机 |
| Track | 车辙 |
| Reflective paint | 反光涂料 |
| Anti-glare panel | 防眩光板 |
| Fatal accident | 重大事故，致亡事故 |
| Fatality rate | 致亡率 |
| Fatal crash | 致亡撞车（事故） |
| Injury crash | 致伤撞车（事故） |
| PDO (property damage only) crash | 仅财产损失的撞车（事故） |
| Alcohol-related accident | 因酒精引起的事故 |
| Drunk-driving control | 酒驾管控 |
| Capped Toll Level | 上限收费水平 |
| Tolling Policy | 过路费收费政策 |

# 第 19 课　高速路运营与养护

## 对话 1

方先生 - 项目公司副总经理

Douglas 先生 - 国家公路管理局副局长

Rock 先生 - 项目公司高速公路养护部经理

Sheriff 先生 - 项目公司高速公路路政部经理

**Douglas 先生**：早上好，方先生。今天你欢迎我这个不速之客吗？

**方先生**：哦，欢迎你，道格拉斯先生。我们永远欢迎您这个尊贵的客人。我能为你做些什么？

**Douglas 先生**：十天前，我收到贵公司关于东西高速公路年度运营的报告。报告说，这条高速公路正在进行常规维护，交通安全得到了很好的保障。为了核实情况，今天我就想去现场检查一下。

**方先生**：我们很乐意随时接受您的检查。您今天准备检查什么？您想从哪里开始检查？

**Douglas 先生**：我不想看报告，而是想直接看到公路养护和运营的真实情况。首先，请让我看一下你们公路养护队的机械设备吧。

**方先生**：我明白了。请允许我介绍一下我们的高速公路养护部经理 Rock 先生和高速公路路政部经理 Sheriff 先生。

**Douglas 先生**：很高兴见到你们，Rock 先生和 Sheriff 先生。

**Rock 先生**：我也是，Douglas 先生。我很荣幸能向您展示我们四个支撑东西高速公路维修的机械站中的一个。您看，这里有两台破碎机、六台反铲挖掘机、八台装载机、十五台自卸车、一台多功能沥青摊铺机、四台振动压路机和一套沥青混凝土搅拌站。

**Douglas 先生**：我相信这些机械大部分是高速公路建设期间使用的吧。你们现在还能让这些机械保持稳定的完好率吗？

**Rock 先生**：是的，我们机械的平均完好率一直保持在90%以上。我们在每个机械站都有一个装备齐全的检修车间，所有的机器都在做定期的精心保养。

**Douglas 先生**：听起来不错啊。那边那台崭新的机器是什么？

**Rock 先生**：那是我们刚从美国购买的一台新的卡特彼勒路面铣刨机。你可能知道，高速公路上有太多的重型车辆超载，把路面压出了很深的路辙。这种路面铣刨机可以在午夜把路面的不平整消除掉，改善某些路段的路面状况，保证第二天一早的交通畅通。

**Douglas 先生**：好棒的机械啊。保持高速公路的交通安全和畅通一直是我们管理局的首要目标。方先生，让我看看你们采取了什么切实的措施来实现这个目标的。

**方先生**：Sheriff 先生，现在轮到你了。

**Sheriff 先生**：好的。我们最好坐上吉普车去看看高速公路沿线的交通安全措施吧。

**Douglas 先生**：好主意。我们走吧。

**方先生**：为了消除人畜进入造成对交通的干扰，我公司在高速公路沿线的某些敏感路段设置了围栏。

**Douglas 先生**：我看见公路边的围栏了。它有效地保障了车流的畅通。

**Sheriff 先生**：我公司对公路交通标识系统进行了升级改造。新的标识能更加明显和系统地提醒司机保持正确的驾驶方式。

**Douglas 先生**：针对夜间行车事故你们有什么措施吗？

**Sheriff 先生**：我们采取了两项措施。一是在高速公路弯道处采用反光涂料；二是在中央护栏上方安装防眩光板。

**Douglas 先生**：你们这些措施的效果如何？

**Sheriff 先生**：相当令人满意。死亡事故大大减少了。去年每 1 亿车公里的死亡率从前年的 8 下降到 6。

**Douglas 先生**：你们在公路安全管理方面做得很好。

**方先生**：但我认为目前的交通事故率仍处于较高水平，包括致亡事故、致伤事故和仅财产损失的事故。统计中，因酒精引起的事故占了大多数。在酒驾管控方面，我们真的需要您的支持哦。

**Douglas 先生**：那当然，国家公路管理局定将尽其所能。

## 对话 2

**Diana 夫人 - 项目公司高速公路收费部经理**

**Roland 先生 - 国家公路管理局收费监管人**

**Diana 夫人**：下午好，Roland 先生。很抱歉今天又来打扰您。

**Roland 先生**：哦，Diana 夫人。你的高速公路通行费收入怎么了？你是不是又要因为交通流量低而申请政府补偿啦？

**Diana 夫人**：不，我今天不是来要求政府补偿的。最近我们高速公路车流量持续增加。但是你看，物价上涨得很快，而我们高速公路收费率长期处于较低水平。我注意到，过去6个月消费者物价指数（CPI）的涨幅超过了15%。把包括偿还银行贷款在内的所有运营成本都考虑在内，在如此低的通行费水平下，甚至连保持正向现金流都不可能。你认为我们公司有理由申请提高收费标准吗？

**Roland 先生**：是的，你说得对。根据《收费公路法》，当最近六个月的 CPI 年增长率超过 25% 时，公路开发商可根据两个条件申请提高收费水平。一是居民消费价格指数自最近一次通行费上调以来涨幅超过 5%；二是所申请的收费水平不应高于该期间的上限收费水平。

**Diana 夫人**：没问题。事实上，我们的收费标准自高速公路开始商业运营以来就一直都没有提高过。我们提高收费一定会依据上限收费水平的。您能解释一下目前的收费上限是多少吗？

**Roland 先生**：上限收费水平是根据收费政策所载的公式计算。我们找个彼此合适的时间，我会告诉你那个公式及如何计算上限收费水平的。

**Diana 夫人**：谢谢您，Roland 先生。请给我一份提高收费水平的申请表好吗？

**Roland**：当然，给你。你可以拿回去填。只要你申请的收费水平是在上限收费水平或以下，我便会根据收费政策和所有相关法律条款予以批准。

**Diana 夫人**：提交申请后多久我们公司可以得到您的批准呢？

**Roland 先生**：这要视情况而定，因为在批准之前我必须得到交通部长的书面许可。

# LESSON 20  HIGHWAY TRANSFER TO THE LOCAL AUTHORITY

**Dialogue**

Mr. Bai-Vice President of Group M and Chairman of International Contracting Company

Mr. Harold-Minister, Ministry of Infrastructure Development

Mr. Fang-General Manager of Project Company

**Mr. Bai:** Good morning, minister. I still remember the former minister Mr. Fernando appointed you to help our group in drafting of Feasibility Study 25 years ago. We will never forget your constant support.

**Mr. Harold:** Good morning, Mr. Bai. I heard about you from Mr. Fernando 25 years ago as well. Time flies. Mr. Fernando is the

Prime Minister of the country right now, and as I know, you are vice president of Group M, aren't you?

**Mr. Bai:** Yes, and I think it is too late to congratulate you've been promoted to the minister of Ministry of Infrastructure Development today. Thank you for taking time off your busy schedule to grant this interview to me. 25-year concession period of West-east Highway is coming to an end in a flash. 16 months ago, we signed a Memorandum on the preparation of West-east Highway transfer. Only 8 months remain for the highway transfer now. Therefore I came from China this time. Today we'd like to report to you our work on the preparation for highway transfer and to discuss the arrangement of the follow-up work before the transfer.

**Mr. Harold:** You came at the right time. Last week, the Prime Minister Mr. Fernando called me and expressing his concern to the transfer of West-east Highway. I am pleased to listen to your report and discuss further arrangement in this regard.

**Mr. Bai:** The newly promoted general manager of West-east Highway Project Company Mr. Fang will make a brief report first.

**Mr. Fang:** After the signing of the Memorandum on the preparation of highway transfer, our project company worked mainly in three aspects, i.e. Final Restorative Overhaul, Fix Assets Inventory and Intellectual Property Summarizing. The restorative overhaul covering 62% road works of whole highway has been completed in accordance of the technical standard attached to the Concession Agreement. An inventory of all the fix assets including vehicles, materials, machinery and affiliated facilities of the highway has been ready for government audit. All the certificates of patent, know-how and right to invention use have been sorted out with the related design documents, confidential data filed.

**Mr. Harold:** Fine. You have done quite a lot for the highway transfer. However, the Concession Agreement was signed 25 years ago, and technology has been greatly developed during this period, especially in electronics techniques and ICT (information & communication technology). I think the restorative overhaul of the traffic control system and toll collecting system should follow new technical standard instead of the old ones.

**Mr. Bai:** I totally agree with you, minister. That's why we have just worked on the road works overhaul up to now. But upgrading of standards of traffic control system and toll collecting system will cause a big expenditure above the budget and beyond the Concession Agreement. We think this should be reasonably compensated by the government.

**Mr. Harold:** Although such compensation will certainly aggravate heavy burden to the stretched finance of the government, I cannot but to admit your request holds water. Please submit updated design of traffic control system and toll collecting system with your compensation suggestion for review and approval within three days.

**Mr. Bai:** Thank you, minister. You will receive our submission in time.

**Mr. Harold:** Mr. Fang, I haven't heard the transfer preparation regarding financial aspects in your report. More attention from the government officials is focusing on the financial status of your project company.

**Mr. Fang:** I understand there is critical concern about the financial issues by the government. Our project company is keeping true, precise and real-time financial record all along with highway operation. Therefore, we can receive government audit to our financial status any time without special preparation. We are looking for government all-round acceptance test and inspection before transfer.

**Mr. Harold:** My ministry is organizing a joint inspection team with government officials, lawyer, CPA (certified public accountant) and test/evaluation professionals. The Treasury will also assign its officials participating the joint inspection team. This team is going to start inspection to your project company two months later.

**Mr. Fang:** Minister, the performance test usually takes quite a long time. I'm really worried about the performance test to the whole 400 more kilometers' highway will hinder the progress of substantive road works transfer. May you assign a professional laboratory to commence the performance test much earlier?

**Mr. Harold:** It seems that your concern is on the right side. When do you think the professional laboratory should start their work on site?

**Mr. Fang:** I would hope they have started performance test yesterday.

**Mr. Harold:** Aha, are you kidding?

**Mr. Fang:** Minister, I was serious but kidding. I'm afraid that the performance test could barely catch up the highway transfer schedule even the professional laboratory would start their work tomorrow.

**Mr. Harold:** I understand that performance test is a matter of urgency. Okay, I will order them to enter your company next week then.

**Mr. Fang:** Thanks for your kind support, minister.

**Mr. Bai:** Minister, I think that training to the staffs of local operation entity is also an important issue. I suggest a name list of the trainees from the local operation entity to be delivered to us within one month, so that our company can work out a specific training course for them.

**Mr. Harold:** How long will it take to train the staffs of local operation entity?

**Mr. Bai:** Usually two months training course and two months' on-the-job internship.

**Mr. Fang:** We hope the potential local operation entity could make an investigation to our project company soon. Since we have already hired quite many local staffs in most of departments, the potential local operation entity just needs to have a small part of the key staffs be trained to replace our Chinese management staffs.

**Mr. Harold:** You are right. I think that most of the local staffs in your company should be hired by the new local operation team. I will order the local operation entity contact you to arrange their investigation and submit a proposed list of trainees as soon as possible. Any other issues from your company need to be discussed today?

**Mr. Bai:** We have no other issue to discuss, minister.

**Mr. Harold:** So, I am going to raise some request to you. The target of our government is to have legal ownership transfer and administrative power transfer of the highway stably and smoothly; ensuring all the assets transferred in good status rather than a burden to the further operation. To achieve this goal, I hope your project company will cooperate with our government closely and friendly.

**Mr. Bai:** No problem. Please believe that we will exert our greatest sincerity and effort to cooperate, minister.

**Mr. Harold:** Well, firstly please submit a Proposal of Highway Transfer Work Plan to me for government consideration and decision.

**Mr. Bai:** Okay, minister. You will find it on your desk early next week.

**Mr. Harold:** And secondly, I need an Assets Inventory of your project company including capital reserve, physical assets, mortgage, guarantee and liabilities. My ministry will forward it to the Treasury for performance appraisal.

**Mr. Bai:** We will submit to you Project Company's Assets Inventory within ten days, Minister.

**Mr. Harold:** Very good. We had a very fruitful meeting today. My secretary will make meeting minutes and distribute it to your company and relevant entities in a couple of days.

## Key-words & Expressions

| | |
|---|---|
| In a flash | 瞬间,一眨眼 |
| Final Restorative Overhaul | 最终恢复性大修 |
| Fix Assets Inventory | 固定资产盘点 |
| Intellectual Property Summarizing | 知识产权汇总 |
| ICT (information & communication technology) | 信息与通信技术 |
| Patent | 专利 |
| Know-how | 专门技术 |
| Right to invention use | 发明使用权 |
| Traffic control system | 交通控制系统 |

| | |
|---|---|
| Toll collecting system | 公路收费系统 |
| Performance test | 性能测试 |
| On-the-job internship | 在职实习 |
| Capital reserve | 资本储备 |
| Physical assets | 实物资产 |

# 第 20 课　向地方当局移交高速路

## 对话

**白先生 - M 集团国际工程承包公司总裁**

**Harold 先生 - 基础设施开发部部长**

**梁先生 - 项目公司总经理**

**白先生：**早上好，部长。我至今还记得前部长 Fernando 先生 25 年前指定您帮助我们集团编制可行性研究呢。我们永远不会忘记您持久不懈的支持。

**Harold 先生：**早上好，白先生。 我在 25 年前就从 Fernando 先生那里知道您。光阴似箭啊。现在 Fernando 是我们国家的总理啦，而据我所知，您是 M 集团的副总裁了，不是吗？

**白先生：**是的。不过我想今天来恭喜您荣升基础设施建设部部长未免太晚了。感谢您在百忙之中抽出时间为我安排这次会面。一眨眼东西高速公路 25 年特许经营期即将结束。16 个月前，我们签署了一份关于东西高速公路移交准备工作的备忘录。现在距高速公路移交只剩下 8 个月了。因此这次我从中国过来。今天，我们打算向您汇报高速公路移交的准备工作，并讨论移交前的后续工作安排。

**Harold 先生：** 您来得正是时候。上周 Fernando 总理打电话给我，表示了对东西高速公路移交的关注。我很高兴听取你们的汇报并讨论这方面的进一步安排。

**白先生：** 首先请东西高速公路项目公司新任总经理方先生作一个简要汇报吧。

**方先生：**《高速公路移交准备备忘录》签署后，我项目公司主要从最终恢复性大修、固定资产盘点、知识产权汇总三个方面开展工作。根据特许经营权协议所附的技术标准，高速公路道路恢复性大修工作已经完成了 62%。高速公路所有固定资产，包括车辆、材料、机械和附属设施的清单已经准备好接受政府审计。所有的专利证书、专有技术证书和发明使用权证书连同相关的设计文件、保密资料均已一并整理归档。

**Harold 先生：** 很好。你们为高速公路移交做了不少工作。然而，特许经营协议是在 25 年前签订的，在此期间技术有了很大的发展，尤其是电子技术和信息与通信技术。我认为交通控制系统和收费系统的恢复性大修应该遵循新的技术标准，而不是旧的。

**白先生：** 我完全同意您的看法，部长。这就是为什么我们至今只对道路工程作了大修。但是，交通控制系统和收费系统标准的升级会产生一大笔超预算的开支，并且是特许经营协议范围之外的。我们认为这应该由政府作合理补偿。

**Harold 先生：** 尽管这样的补偿无疑会加重政府捉襟见肘的财政负担，但我不得不承认您的要求是站得住脚的。请你们在三天内提交新版交通管制系统和收费系统的设计以及你们的补偿建议以供审批。

**白先生**：谢谢您，部长。您会如期收到我们的提案。

**Harold 先生**：方先生，我在你的报告中没有听到关于财务方面的移交准备。政府官员更关注的是你们项目公司的财务状况。

**方先生**：我理解政府非常关注财务问题。项目公司在高速公路运营过程中始终保持着真实、准确、实时的财务记录。因此，我们可以随时接受政府对我们财务状况的审计而无需特别准备。我们期待着政府的全方位验收测试和移交前视察。

**Harold 先生**：我部正在组织一个由政府官员、律师、注册会计师和测试/评估专业人员组成的联合检查组。财政部也将指派官员参加联合检查组。这个小组将在两个月后开始对你们的项目公司进行检查。

**方先生**：部长，性能测试通常需要花费很长时间。我真的很担心 400 多公里的高速公路的性能测试会拖累高速公路工程移交的实质性进展。您可否安排一个专业实验室更早开始性能测试吗？

**Harold 先生**：看来你的担心是对的。你认为专业实验室应该什么时候开始现场工作？

**方先生**：我希望他们昨天就能开始性能测试。

**Harold 先生**：啊哈，你是在开玩笑吧？

**方先生**：部长，我不是开玩笑而是认真的。恐怕即便专业实验室明天就开始工作，性能测试也仅能勉强赶上高速公路移交时间表。

**Harold 先生**：我理解性能测试是一项紧急的事务。好吧，那我让他们下周就进驻你们公司。

**方先生**：谢谢您的支持，部长。

**白先生**：部长，我认为对本地运营实体的员工进行培训也是一个重要的问题。我建议在一个月内将本地运营实体的受训人员名单交给我们，以便我们公司为他们制定一套特定的培训课程。

**Harold 先生**：培训本地运营实体的员工需要多长时间？

**白先生**：通常是两个月的培训课程加两个月的在职实习。

**方先生**：我们希望潜在的当地运营实体能尽快对我们的项目公司进行调研。由于我们已经在大多数部门雇用了相当多的本地员工，潜在的本地运营实体只需要培训一小部分关键员工来取代我们的中国管理人员。

**Harold 先生**：你说得对。我认为贵公司大部分的本地员工应该由新的本地运营团队雇用。我会命令本地运营实体尽快联系你来安排他们调研，并提交一份拟受训人员名单。今天你们公司还有其他问题需要讨论吗？

**白先生**：我们没有其他问题了，部长。

**Harold 先生**：那我要向你们提出一些要求了。我国政府的目标是使高速公路的合法所有权和管理权得以平稳、顺利地移交，确保所有移交的资产处于良好的状态，而不是成为进一步经营的负担。为了实现这一目标，我希望贵项目公司与我国政府密切、友好合作。

**白先生**：没有问题。请相信我们会尽最大的诚意和努力来合作，部长先生。

**Harold 先生**：嗯，首先请向我提交一份高速公路移交工作计划的建议稿以供政府考虑和决策。

**白先生：** 好的，部长。下周初您会在您的桌子上看到它的。

**Harold 先生：** 其次，我需要一份贵项目公司的资产清单，包括资金储备、实物资产、抵押、担保和负债。我部将把它转交给财政部进行绩效评估。

**白先生：** 部长，我们将在十天内向您提交项目公司的资产清单。

**Harold 先生：** 很好。我们今天开了一个富有成效的会议。我的秘书会做一份会议纪要，并在几天内分发给贵公司和相关实体。